Buddy Baer
Autobiography

Rhino Publishing, S.A.

Buddy Baer
Autobiography

Copyright, 2003

All rights reserved. Copyright under Berne Copyright Convention, Universal Copyright Convention, and Pan-American Copyright Convention. No part of this book may be reproduced, stored in a retrieval system, or transmitted in any form, or by any means, electronic, mechanical, photocopying, recording or otherwise, without prior written permission of the publisher and author.

ISBN 9962-636-59-0

RHINO PUBLISHING, S.A.
World Trade Center
Panama, Republic of Panama
Voicemail/Fax
International: + 416-352-5126
North America: 888-317-6767

ACKNOWLEDGEMENTS

I am indebted to many people for the good life I have led, but here I wish to thank a few who forced me to relive portions of the past for the purpose of this book: Michael Douglas of the California State Employees Association, for pushing me into the endeavor; Vicki, my wife, who tolerated numerous recorded interview sessions in our kitchen, added insights of her own, and collected and organized what remains of my news clippings and pictures; Frances and Bernice, my sisters, who prodded my memory and helped with the interviews; Eddie Lopez, book editor of the <u>Fresno Bee,</u> who found valuable history in the files of his paper; the staff in the morgue at the <u>Oakland Tribune,</u> who allowed us to poke around in their files; Minny Maderis, a family friend in Livermore who contributed her memories; and Johnny Smith, an old friend from school days who remembered events I had forgotten.

Contents

A CROWN MISPLACED	9
MAX IN BLOOM (AGE 3)	21
CALIFORNIA BECKONS	31
WILD WEST ON THE BAY	41
MAX UNTAMED	51
BANNED IN CALIFORNIA	61
HELLO BROADWAY	71
ONWARD, UPWARD, OOPS	87
LIFE IN THE FAST LANE	107
THE BEST OF TIMES	117
FROM LITTLE TO BIG BROTHER	143
PROFESSIONAL PROTECTION	161
I BELIEVE	167
THE BARITONE AFFAIR	175
THE YEAR THAT WASN'T	179
THE BATTLES OF BRITAIN	183
TREADING WATER	197
THE MOON AND THE MOUNTAIN	215
IMPRESSING THE PRESS	225
OUR LAST FIGHTS	235
BEDTIME FOR BUDDY	247
CAMERA, LIGHTS, ACTION	253
LADY LUCK DROPS	277
HER HANDKERCHIEF	277
REFLECTIONS	285
EPITAPH	291
MEMORABILIA	293

A CROWN MISPLACED

It is spring, 1984, forty-three years after the event that foreshadowed the end of my boxing career, and I have not changed my mind. I should have been the second of the brothers Baer to have won the heavyweight championship of the world.

I say this with due humility, for I have never claimed to be one of the all-time great boxers. And I do think that my opponent on that fateful night of May 23, 1941, Joe Louis, was probably the best of all heavyweights up to that time and even up to now. But the facts are clear. In that particular fight I should have been declared the technical winner on a foul. In truth, it was a double foul. Such a decision would have given me the championship, and I think I would have held it longer than my brother Max did.

It was the first of my two fights with Joe. The place was Griffith Stadium in Washington, D.C., better known as the home of the Washington Senators baseball team, which seldom drew the kind of crowd we had that night. The papers said more than 30,000 were on hand. That was close to capacity. And I could feel in my bones that at least half of those fans were pulling for me to upset the champion.

I was a 10 to 1 betting underdog, but judging from the roar that came from those 30,000 throats when we entered the ring, I knew that the betting odds (10-1 Louis) did not reflect the crowd's belief in my ability to win. After all, I had won 49 of my 53 previous fights, and just six weeks earlier I had knocked out "Beer Barrel" Tony Galento, the most famous fistic brawler of the time.

On top of that, I outweighed Joe by 32 pounds and had a six-inch reach advantage. In short, I had the necessary physical equipment and a good enough fighting record to justify the crowd's hope that I could destroy the legend of invincibility that had grown up around Joe Louis Barrows. In my own mind, I knew I could do it, just as Max Schmeling had done four years earlier.

No fighter ever approaches the ring alone. When I came down the aisle in Griffith Stadium, Ancil Hoffman, my manager, Izzy Klein, my trainer, and Ray Arcel, my cut man accompanied me. It was a long walk. Each step we took seemed to generate ever-higher decibel counts of noise from the sea of faces around us. When I crawled through the ropes and began my warm-up dance in my corner of the ring, the din actually hurt my ears.

Ancil and Izzy shouted instructions, but I couldn't hear them. Their lips moved furiously but soundlessly. Then Joe and his entourage made their entrance, and a fresh wave of acoustical uproar rolled across the playing field, engulfing the arena in which we would momentarily perform. (Years later I would be reminded of this scene when I played the role of a gladiator in the movie, Quo Vadis, which seemed to be a replay of the real thing. Joe Louis was just as fearsome as any lion, and the fight crowd was just as bloodthirsty as the mobs in ancient Roman amphitheaters.)

Now Joe was in his corner, doing his own little warm-up by jogging in place, staring past me and seemingly into space. I thought about my battle plan, which was to attack, attack, attack... Use my weight and reach to force Joe backward, into the ropes, into the corners...Don't let him get set, or I get hurt... Respect his lethal power, fight close in, move out of range fast, move back close, tie him up, and hit on the break. The bell rang.

We met in center ring. Joe immediately grazed my chin with a left jab and I countered with five or six rights and lefts to his body. He backed away, jabbing constantly with his left. I pursued him with two swings that missed. He tried to catch me off balance and missed with his first right of the fight. I nailed him on his neck with a left hook before he regained his balance, and he then let loose a combination of lefts and rights to my head that produced a fleeting vision of shooting stars and roman candles.

But my head cleared almost instantly and I moved forward again, throwing more leather than I can remember in detail. Joe had his back against the ropes when I caught him high on his cheekbone with my best-left hook, smashing his body between the two upper strands of rope. He somersaulted out of the ring, striking the apron with his head.

To me, being out of the ring was the same as being down, so I returned to my corner and watched Joe get up and step toward the crowd. He was dazed enough to be turned completely around. One more step and he would have landed in the press section five or more feet below, and, unlike Dempsey when Firpo actually propelled him into the press row and he was pushed by the reporters back into the ring, Joe might not have negotiated that maneuver in time. But he caught himself before the fatal step, turned, and crawled back through the ropes at the count of four.

My memory is vague on when Arthur Donovan, the referee, actually started the count, but I have since thought that he must have been very slow. Is it really possible to be slammed through the ropes, land on your head, rise to your feet and take two steps away from the ring, turn around and crawl back, all in just four seconds? I have always questioned Mr. Donovan's count, but this is the first time I have put it in writing.

In any case, later events pushed this matter into oblivion as a technicality not worth consideration. "So what if Joe really used nine counts to get back, he got back in time, didn't he?" was the general consensus. I agree with the consensus, but the technicality just added to my doubts about Mr. Donovan later on.

I tried and unfortunately failed to put Joe away when fighting resumed. Before the round ended he delivered a ferocious wallop to my rib cage, and I could see in his eyes that he had regained his composure and fighting intensity. I thought to myself, though, that I had taken some of his best shots and I still felt clearheaded and strong. My battle plan still seemed sound.

The second round was another story. Joe broke through my defense time after time with short, quick blows that forced me backward. It was just the opposite of what I wanted to do. I managed to counter with a few punches that I knew were not effective. Joe's punches hurt, but so far they weren't living up to his reputation as a killer. He won the round, easily, and we were even on that score.

Round three was much the same as the second, but in the fourth I landed a solid right on Joe's mouth that snapped his head back and brought a quick look of alarm to his eyes. I tried to follow through, but he deftly sidestepped my right and blocked my left jabs. Soon he was on the attack, delivering painful smashes to my head and body. Score now, I realized, was three rounds to one in favor of Joe, but I was still strong and confident that I could knock him out if only I could reach his chin with a fully powered right.

One of the most frequent questions I have been asked since I left the fight game is "what do your seconds say to you between rounds when you are losing on points?" Izzy told me after the fourth round of this fight to "stay away! Force him!" A neat trick, to go backward and forward at the same time. But I knew what he meant. I should do a better job of ducking and evading, then step forward and blast away. In the fifth it worked to an extent. Joe threw a right hand that cut a path through my hair as I got under it, then I came up with a left hook to his left eye that clearly hurt him. He dabbed at the eye with his glove and saw blood. "Is this really happening to me?" he seemed to say to himself. In just a few seconds the eye began to swell and turn red. Though I didn't really have the stomach for it, I tried to follow the boxer's credo that an injury should be the target. Joe proved again that he could be very elusive, and I could not take advantage of his difficulty. However, I thought the round was pretty even.

Not so the sixth. Joe came out firing, which surprised me, for I thought he would be too tired to do that after hitting me with so many punches, and missing with so many too, in the five previous rounds.

Looking back, I am convinced that he had become worried about my punching power. He was afraid that he just might catch a knockout blow if he didn't finish the fight soon. He rushed out and immediately rained a series of hooks and uppercuts to my head, arms and body. Maybe it was the adrenaline that moved him to such fury, but he was throwing harder punches now than in the beginning. A lightning right caught my chin. I started to go down. Stories the next day said that I twisted downward like a leaf from a tree, which was an accurate description of my sensation of falling.

Instinct guided me. When I settled on the canvas, stomach down, I managed to get my knees under me and rise to be greeted again with a volley of blows. This time I landed on my back, and took as much time as I could. At the count of nine I was up, and flicked a weak left jab as Joe swarmed all over me at the bell.

I turned and walked toward my corner, reeling slightly. When things are going badly it's funny how much can flash through your mind in a couple of seconds. At this moment I was thinking of cold water splashing over my head and shoulders when I reached my corner. That and a one-minute rest would be enough to put me back in shape for the seventh round. Suddenly, the lights almost went out. I found myself back on the canvas, rolling over and trying to crawl to my feet. I had been hit, from behind, by the strongest blow of the fight.

I saw two of everything the lights above, the ringposts, Ancil, Izzy, Donovan, Joe. Faces in the crowd gyrated dizzily. I almost threw up, but instead, somehow, I got up. Griffith Stadium was in a wild uproar. Dozens of reporters were on their feet screaming, "foul.' foul!" Ancil and Izzy were all over Donovan, claiming the obvious, that I had been hit after the bell. Donovan was pushing them back to the corner. The bell rang for round seven and I started to move out, but was pulled back by Ancil and Izzy. They shouted at Donovan that I should have extra time because of the late hit, but Donovan refused, and Joe came out to fight. When my corner continued to hold me back, Donovan walked over to Louis, raised his am, and declared him the winner.

Now, I do not relish winning a fight on a foul. But there are rules. Joe broke two of them when he unloaded on me after the bell, and when his blow landed at the back of my left ear a rabbit punch. Either one should have disqualified him, but Donovan chose instead to disqualify me, on grounds that my handlers would not let me start the seventh round. It was true; they wouldn't, unless I had time to recover from the fouls. The rules plainly state that if the foul is not in itself considered to be disqualifying, the victim is to have five extra minutes to recover from its effects. If I had done the same thing to Joe, I would have expected to either lose the fight then and there, or to see him granted the five-minute recovery period.

Maybe Joe didn't hear the bell. I'll allow him that. I'll also grant that any fighter, when he senses imminent victory and in the excitement of the moment, can lose his judgment enough to deliver an illegal punch. Joe did just that, but I blame him for the outcome a lot less than I blame the officials for failing to do their duty. By ignoring a flagrant violation of the rules, they failed to protect me, failed to protect the sport of boxing, and failed to protect the right of boxing fans to see a fair fight.

One of the two judges did try to do his job. Jimmy Sullivan voted to disqualify Louis for hitting after the bell, and he hotly maintained his position during the next several days of controversy over the decision. But he was outnumbered by the combination of the second judge and Donovan, the referee.

Later, I learned from Sec Taylor, a sports writer for the Des Moines Register, that Donovan was on the payroll of Mike Jacobs, who promoted most of Louis' fights, and that Jacobs owned 10 percent of Louis. He was sitting next to Jacobs when I belted Louis out of the ring. According to Taylor, Jacobs' upper denture fell from his mouth, and he shouted loud enough for many around him to hear, "there goes my meal ticket!"

Another aspect of Jacobs' operation that always bothered me was the use of Donovan as the referee in all 24 of Louis' last fights, including 19 title defenses. Donovan was not the only qualified referee in the country. There were many others. The fact that Jacobs always chose Donovan tends to support my belief that Jacobs thought he could depend on Donovan in a close situation. In my case that certainly proved to be true. But Louis, of all fighters, did not need that kind of insurance. Even so, it looks to me as though Jacobs decided not to take any chances.

I don't know if there was a law at the time prohibiting a promoter from owning a piece of a fighter in bouts he was promoting. I don't know if there was a law that prohibited referees from being on the promoter's payroll. But I do know that it wasn't ethical. I have said many times since my boxing career ended that fight promoters and financiers usually have only two things in mind, petty and grand larceny.

I'll agree that my brother, Max, who heard that fight on the radio at his home in Sacramento, was not an objective interpreter of what happened, but I like what he said to reporters that night. "I can't understand why a fighter has to go into the ring, fight Louis, the two judges, the referee and the announcer. Buddy got the works. This is the first time I heard of a champion getting his eye cut and having it affect his hearing." He said it better then than I can now.

As I said at the beginning, I think that if I had been awarded the title (just as Schmeling had been when he was fouled by Jack Sharkey), I would have held it longer than did my brother Max. He loved high living more than he loved boxing. He had the talent to have been as good as or even better than any other heavyweight in history, but he frittered away his opportunities on a diet of fast night life, happy high jinks and plain non-stop fun. Because I was younger and trying to follow in his footsteps as a boxer I would have benefited by his mistakes.

And please, don't get me wrong on the matter of high living, which I enjoyed just as much as Max did. As things turned out, I may have indulged in more of it than he did, but that was mostly after I quit boxing. If I had won the title, I would have behaved enough to be in shape. I would have fought frequently, as Louis was doing. Eventually, of course, I would have given Joe another match, as he did for me, but for reasons I will explain later, the outcome would not have been a first round knockout. (Joe KO'd me in less than three minutes in our second fight.) Maybe he would have beaten me, but not that easily.

In the meantime, I am sure I could have handled the other challengers. Probably Lou Nova was the best of the lot, with the possible exception of Tommy Farr. Nova gave Max a thrashing. Not many fighters did that. I wanted to fight Lou, but he steadfastly refused, and for good reason. He knew that I could beat him.

His perception of that fact came about this way. We both used Jimmy Duffy's Gym in Oakland, California, for our training. One day I suggested that we do a couple rounds of sparring. He agreed. After a minute or so he threw his best right at my head, with all of his power behind it. He clearly intended to knock me out. I ducked it easily, and finished the round without countering in kind. But in the second round he tried another KO punch with his left, which missed, and I caught him a blistering crack on his jaw with my right. He went down like a steer from the blow of an axe. He was not unconscious, but if there had been a referee he would not have made it up in ten. I had turned the tables on Mr. Nova, for it had been his clear intention to flatten me and then let the world know that he had given me the same treatment he dished out to Max. It didn't work, and I did not announce to anyone what had happened, simply because I hoped that Lou would give me a fight. But I defeated my purpose, Lou's memory of that punch stayed with him for the rest of his boxing career. He always found a reason to deny me a fight.

Nova didn't actually flatten Max, but he did give him a first rate boxing lesson and cut him up quite thoroughly in the process. I was at ringside for this fight and observed the proceedings carefully, after all, I might fight him later. It was plain to see that Lou was a boxing artist who moved in circles, using every inch of ring space, luring his opponent into wild swings and quickly countering with hooks and uppercuts. So it was with Max. He wore my brother down, first by letting him tire himself, and then peppering his head and body with jolting jabs. His best punch was ordinarily not lethal, but he landed with regularity. At the end, Max was exhausted and beaten. His face resembled freshly cut round steak.

I was a much better boxer than Max. I wouldn't have let Nova do to me what he did to Max. My best punch was just as hard as Max's (and his was as hard as any the experts had ever seen), and there is no doubt in my mind that I would have landed it on Nova's chin if I had ever had the chance. I would have knocked him out.

Would I have been an enduring champion, with the likes of Joe Louis waiting for a rematch? While I think the answer might well be "yes," I would like it to be understood that the question is of secondary importance to me. The main question remains "was the wrong fighter disqualified on May 23, 1941?" The record suggests strongly that the answer is "yes."

MAX IN BLOOM (AGE 3)

I dearly loved my brother. So did my sisters. So did everyone who really knew him. From the beginning of my memory of him he was fun loving, full of laughter, friendly to all and loyal to his friends. To say that Max was unique may be saying too much, but he came as close to being one of a kind as the nature of humanity will permit.

One of the many titles bestowed on him by the press was "clown prince." It was a title he shared with John Barrymore, a stage and movie actor of international standing, whose off-stage and off-screen adventures were as well known as the roles he portrayed. Max was cut from the same cloth. He was an actor in the ring and out. But unlike Barrymore, he always played himself.

The image that Max projected around the world was that of a care-free, irrepressible, fun-loving Greek god who, when he could put 60 serious minutes together in sequence, was unconquerable in the ring, and out of the ring was a dashing bon vivant and a lover of monumental proportions. I do not argue with the accuracy of that image, though I hasten to add that the image was in black and white. The reality of Brother Max was in living, blazing Technicolor!

Our grandfather, Aschill Baer, was a French Jew from Alsace-Lorraine who migrated to America as a youth. Not long after his arrival he saw a photo of Fanny Fischel, of Vienna, in a friend's picture album and was smitten. He paid her way to come over here and marry him. She bore him seven sons, one of whom was our father, Jacob Henry, and two daughters. The sons were named for the tribes of Israel, and all were given their early education in Jewish schools.

Despite this impressive recognition of his Jewish heritage, Aschill and Fanny did not insist on any of their children following the Jewish faith if they wished to do otherwise. This paved the way for our parents (Dad married Dora Bales, of Scotch-Irish ancestry) to live independent of any particular faith, and to give Max and me and our sisters the freedom to decide on a religion when we wanted to, then, later or never. We grew up respecting our Jewish connection, but were completely unconcerned about that religion or any other. Though Max was

*Papa And Mama Baer
(Jake And Dora)
on their wedding day
in Omaha,
Christmas eve, 1904.*

not a bookworm, he did think of himself as a worm. I think of him as a classic case of the worm that turned.

Max was proud of this sketch, done by one of the nation's foremost illustrators.

All these years later I still meet people across the country who were young when Max was young, who say he was their idol. Women, because of his masculine magnificence and sparkling humor; men because of his fighting ability and personal style. But it was a different story back in 1922, in Durango, Colorado, a mining and cow town of the Old West that hadn't quite lost the vestiges of its past. Our family had moved there from Denver at the end of World War I. Max had just turned 13 and I was nearly eight and old enough to remember that Max was vastly different from the image he was to develop in later years. He was not a budding Greek God. Biologically, he was old enough, but he was not a lover. He was shy, something of a loner, more of an introvert than anyone in the family.

I remember that he was tall for his age, but thin. His cheekbones accentuated his long, triangular face, which sloped downward over slightly depressed cheeks to a strong, jutting jaw. It was his mouth that betrayed the future Max, curving waspishly at the corners, giving him a look of steady bemusement. As I look at his early pictures in our family album today I would guess, if I didn't know better, that he whiled away his time with books.

He did seem to know something about the rest of us that he thought was funny. He never took himself or anyone seriously. He found a lot to laugh about. Much of it was within, for he would suddenly chuckle to himself, or even break out in loud laughter, while the family was eating silently at the dinner table. When Dad would ask, "What's so funny Max?" his inevitable answer was "nothing."

Growing up in Durango was not easy for boys who didn't like to fight. The town had a history of frontier violence. Many living residents were a part of that history, and they told stories of blazing shootouts and heroic fisticuffs that kept alive the idea that the quickest, fairest way to settle an argument was to fight it out. I'm sure that every town in America, then and now, has bred a number of young men for whom that idea is very appealing; but Durango had more than its fair share. Max was not one of them, and that fact led to his own opinion of himself as a coward, a worm.

Our parents were against needless violence and what Dad called "street brawling." Now Dad was a real tough guy, so he spoke from a position of strength when he advised Max to steer clear of brawls that had no other purpose than to elevate some macho character in the eyes of his peers (I was not included because of my tender age). Dad, after all, could have been a very good professional boxer. He went 22 rounds one time with Jim Jeffries while he was in training to see if he was good enough to fight for a living. He also went a lot of rounds with Tom Sharkey, but decided in the end that the paychecks were more regular and more certain in the slaughterhouse work he knew as well as anybody in the business. He could kill, skin and butcher a steer faster than any man in the country. All of us in the family were very proud of the record he set in the Denver stockyard when he transformed a raging 1,300-pound bull into steaks and chops in just three minutes and 36 seconds.

Dad's manly credentials were much in order. So were his other credentials-gentleness, warmth, generosity and a loving nature. When he told us what was right and wrong, we listened. On the day that he told Max it was right to walk away from situations that could lead to a pointless fight, and wrong to let anyone take advantage of him, Max heard the first part but not the second.

Mother was just as important an influence on Max's early attitude about fighting as Dad. " I work too hard to keep you in decent clothes to have you come home in tatters from some stupid fight," she warned him. "You show up here all dirty and torn and you'll get a worse lickin than you can get on the street." With variations on the theme, she delivered that message to Max over and over again.

As it happened, Max was good in team sports. For one so young he threw a baseball very hard and accurately, fielded more surely than any of his teammates, and kept opposition fielders on the run with the power of his hits. He was almost as good in football and basketball. Jealousy was bound to arise among some of the roughs, who couldn't figure out why Max was so good on the playing field and such a stand-offish guy everywhere else, and it did. A gang of these toughs decided to push him into a fight.

One afternoon Max was walking home from school with two friends, a boy and a girl. "Smokey" Blackstone (I shall call him) ran up from behind, trailed by several companions, and stepped in front of Max "What makes you think you can get away with my girl? he demanded. The girl quickly told Smokey that she did not know him and to get lost. Instead, he grabbed Max by the front of his shirt, shoved him backward, and put up his fists. Smokey's friends gathered around in a circle, pulling the girl and Max's other friend into their ranks.

The prospective fighters were enclosed. Max looked Smokey in the eyes and said, "You're crazy, go to hell!" With that he turned, burst through the circle and took off for home, not stopping until he was safely in the kitchen.

That was the first time Max ran from a fight, but not the last. Word got around that he was a pushover for any pool hall artist who wished to advance his tough guy image. Max obliged many times, always running when challenged, always thinking he was doing the right thing. I was in the second grade at the time and Max was in the eighth a world apart for kids in those age groups-but the older boys broke the age barrier and deigned to talk to me about my brother. What they wanted to know was why Max was so good in sports and so lousy as a fighter. I answered that Max could beat any two of them at a time if he wanted to, but he was to kind.

Our oldest sister, Frances, age 15 at the time, should have been the family boxer. She is the one who got in the middle of Max's numerous fracases and saved his clothing as well as his face from excessive wear and tear. One time when she was engaged in one of these enterprises, trying to keep kids from giving my brother a working over, one of them kicked her hard in the stomach. She dropped to her knees and began to vomit. This frightened the marauders, who immediately left the scene. But Frances knew who had done it, and told our parents the story that evening. Dad went to see the boy's father, to let him know what kind of a warrior he had for a son. The father was furious, and after the boy admitted his misdeed, gave him a whipping that Dad said could be heard a block away. In Durango, hitting a woman or a girl was as close to the ultimate sin as one could get.

The worm turned one spring afternoon after school. Frances was at home doing homework. She looked out the bay window and saw Max dash into the yard with a boy on his heels. Max stumbled and fell and the boy leaped on him, flailing away at his head with both fists. She raced into the yard, pulled the boy off, slapped him across the face and screamed, " You dirty coward, why don't you pick on someone your own size!" The attacker, who in reality was smaller than Max (who was nearly six feet), quickly, backed away, as Dad came out the door. "What in God's name is going on here?' he demanded of Max. Max lowered his eyes, but Frances responded, " I don't know, but I do know that they're always picking on Max and he won't fight back. I'm tired of getting involved when he refuses to help himself, and I'm not going to do it anymore!" With that she marched off into the house.

Dad was aghast. "Won't fight back?" he roared. "A son of mine won't fight back when attacked in your own yard. Are you sick, Max? Max finally looked up. " I guess I am sick" he said. Í can't seem to avoid a fight without running and the more I run the more I feel like a coward. That's what makes me sick."

"You ought to feel sick," Dad shot back. "I thought you were old enough to know the difference between avoiding a fight that isn't worth fighting and running from a fight that can't be avoided! Get to your room and I'll talk to you later."

Frances remembers it well. Dad then took Mother aside and told her that she was making Max into a coward by insisting that he stay out of fights to keep his clothes clean. Mother said that maybe she had gone too far, but that he (Dad) was even more responsible because he hadn't made it clear to Max what he meant when he advised against getting into the gutter with ruffians. "Max is likely to listen to his father on such matters a lot more than he will to me," she said. "I'll tell Max that his clothes aren't worth the price he's paying, and you tell him what you want to tell him"

Dad did lecture Max, telling him, in effect, to fight when fired upon. A new Max emerged. The very next day a gang of his regular tormentors told him that they didn't like his present appearance, that they would like to rearrange his facial features, that he had better start fighting if he wanted to shed his cowardly reputation. He surprised the hell out of them by agreeing to beat them up one at a time. "We'll go some place where we have witnesses, and I'll start with you George. That should take about five seconds. Then you, Mike. Another five seconds. As for you, Pete, I can hardly wait to remove your teeth. Anybody else is welcome. Let's go."

They didn't go. One by one they turned and went the other way. So Max, just a few weeks before we moved away from Durango, lost his coward's image, and, more importantly, improved his opinion of himself. All without laying a hand on anyone.

CALIFORNIA BECKONS

Frances had been suffering from rheumatic fever all the time we lived in Durango. Dad was bothered by high blood pressure. He was far more concerned about Frances than about himself, and blamed the long, bitter Durango winters for making her condition worse. Situated in the Rocky Mountains at an elevation of 6,500 feet, the little town of 1,200 souls was buried in snow and ice from early November to mid-April, and seemed to be directly in the path of every arctic blast that whistled through and across the peaks and valleys of southern Colorado. The winter of 1921-22 was the last Dad wanted to see in such a place. We had relatives in California who invited us to come and live with them until we could resettle in our own place.

Mother was in full agreement that we pull stakes and go west. She shared Dad's confidence that he could get a job anywhere, and more importantly, she felt he would live longer and that Frances might finally get over the painful rheumatic attacks that were making her life miserable.

But the decision to leave Durango was not easy. There were friends we probably would not see again, long-distance travel being a major undertaking in those days. Dad liked his job at the Gradon Mercantile Company, and then there were the beautiful months of May through October, which even California might not be able to match. And getting all the way to the Pacific would pose problems the family had never before faced.

Always in the past, when the family moved from city to city, it had been at the expense of the Swift Meatpacking Company, which employed Dad to manage various branches of their far-flung livestock empire. The company shipped all of our furniture and household belongings by train to the new destination, and we followed in the comfort of Union Pacific or Southern Pacific passenger cars.

Frances and Max were the only Baer kids who had been born when the family made its first such trip from Omaha to Denver in 1910. Max was only one year old, but Frances was five and smart enough to be 10. Her alert, retentive mind took in all the new and dazzling experiences, beginning with the Omaha railroad station. "It was the biggest building I had ever seen by far," she recalls. "Pictures on the wall were as high as a house and so long that they faded out of sight in the vast distances of the waiting room. I know now that they were murals, but then I knew only that they were the most beautiful paintings I had ever seen. The city of Omaha was shown at one end, the Pacific Ocean at the other, and in between was the prairie, the mountains and the desert. If it still exists, and if I could see it again, I'm sure that I would be just as thrilled now as I was then."

The train was best of all. I had never traveled any faster than a horse could pull a buggy, so the sensation of moving at speeds of up to 90 miles an hour was the most exciting thing of my life. We passed through entire towns and saw only blurs of stores, houses and people in the streets. We flashed past enormous herds of cattle in just seconds, and one time a couple of cowboys raced us, waving their hats as they disappeared from view. The dining car was elegant beyond anything in my experience. Each table was decorated with freshly cut flowers, sparkling white linen tablecloths and gleaming silverware. When I picked up my fork I almost dropped it, it was so heavy! The waiter put on a show each time he served me, calling me 'Lady Baer' and bowing as if I were royalty. It was wonderful."

The family stayed in Denver long enough for Bernice and me to make our appearance, then Dad was transferred to a tiny place in New Mexico called Kaylor. It had a permanent population of less than 100, which doubled whenever cattle drives ended there and the cowboys settled down for a few days of fun. Dad's job, of course, was to run the slaughterhouse that provided Kaylor with its only employment. I was an infant, so I have no memories of the place at all, but Bernice was four and she remembers seeing rattlesnakes climbing up the screen door in our kitchen. Frances says Bernice remembers well. "In the early morning, rattlers came to where it was warm. Our kitchen was the warmest place in the house. If we weren't careful, they would get inside. Dad killed every rattler he saw in or around the house, but there was more than enough to replace them, and the rattler problem was never solved."

One day Frances went on an overnight trip with Dad and several cowboys to look at some cattle being offered for sale. Dad and Frances slept in a wagon, but the others rolled up in their blankets on the ground. When one of the cowboys awoke the next morning he found a rattler curled up on his chest. He was afraid to move, or even speak, and didn't. He lay there, hardly daring to breathe, until one of his buddies got up and saw the situation. He took careful aim with his rifle, steadying his elbow on a nearby boulder, and blew the rattler's head off. The shot awakened everybody, and when Frances looked out of the wagon she saw a bloody cowboy jumping up and down on the remains of the snake while the one who killed it was rolling over and over on the ground, screaming with laughter. The enraged cowboy's blood was not his own, but the snake's.

Coyotes and wolves were as much a part of the New Mexico landscape as the distant blue mesas. For them, life was good and bountiful as long as it lasted. One coyote could kill a calf. Two big wolves could bring down a steer. Between them, they cost ranchers a lot of money, and were hunted relentlessly. Wolves were hard to catch, but coyotes died by the hundreds in our area, and each one was hung by its tail to a fence mainly as a warning to live coyotes, but partly out of hatred for the beasts.

There was no school in Kaylor, so Frances was sent away to a boarding school in Denver. After a year of this Mother and Dad were so upset over having the family split that we are returned to Denver and stayed until our move to Durango in 1919. Being a butcher in those days meant that if you were good you could get a job just about any place you chose to go provided there was a slaughterhouse in the area. As I've said, Dad was very good at his job, good enough that he nearly always had offers to take other jobs. When the Gradon Mercantile Company offered him better pay to manage the meat side of their business, it was "goodbye Denver, hello Durango."

These wheels wouldn't have suited Max, but they were just fine for his father Jake, front, his Uncle Ben, Mack and two unidentified men in the rear. Photo probably taken in 1911, outside Denver.

    Dad bought his first car while we were in Durango. I've forgotten the make, but I remember its style, an open two seat touring car with pull-up top and isinglass sides that buttoned into place. Like all cars of the day, it was black, and in our eyes, magnificent. When the decision was made to leave Durango and go to California, Dad announced that we would ship our furniture by train, and drive the thousand or more miles in our new ship of the desert.

Mother and Dad sat in front with the four of us kids in the back. We pulled out of Durango on a warm, sunny day in May 1922, leaving behind the only paved road we would see for the next several days. Cruising along at 40 to 50 miles an hour, the wind caressing our faces and tousling our hair, we had never been happier. Dad, who chewed tobacco, let fly every few minutes with a spurt of juice aimed at the side of the road, but the wind carried it dangerously near the back seat. We quickly learned to lean to the right on these occasions, and given the weight of Frances, Max and Bernice, plus little me, the car tilted heavily. The scene would have made a good Mack Sennett comedy, with the camera following our car swaying and lurching into the sunset.

Western roads in 1922 were patched up wagon tracks. At their best they were covered with gravel to a width of two cars, but that didn't prevent the formation of deep ruts and the build-up of gravel between the tracks. There were times when we thought our oil pan would be torn loose as we passed over the higher ridges. To avoid such a catastrophe, Dad tried driving between the ruts and nearly flipped us over when the loose gravel gave way. From then on we stayed in the ruts, just as if we were back in a horse-drawn wagon.

This luxurious road gave way to hard-packed desert sand at the New Mexico border. Nothing had been done to alter its surface or width since the introduction of the internal combustion engine. We were driving on the same road that had been traversed by covered wagons, and in dry weather it was smooth and excellent. I wonder, however, whether it was usable at all in wet weather. Fortunately, we were spared the necessity of finding out.

In the back trunk we carried a tent, canned food, water and extra gas for emergencies. Gas was available along the way at small general stores many miles apart. Each store had a single pump, hand operated, and there was only one kind of gas because all cars used the same mixture. At night we pitched our tent in the vicinity of one of these stores. If we were lucky we could buy fresh meat for dinner, but usually that delicacy was not available and we had to be content with corned or dried meat to go with our beans and coffee. Mother and Frances refused to sleep in the tent for fear of snakes. They stayed in the car. We encouraged their fear for it would have been a tight fit in the tent if they had chosen otherwise.

Halfway across Arizona's baking desert we hit a stretch of sand that had blown across the road, skidded completely around, bounced into a roadside rock, and broke the front axle. Dad turned off the engine, and there we were, in the middle of an overwhelmingly silent emptiness, with the blazing sun nearing its mid-day zenith, stranded.

The situation was serious, and Dad knew it. We hadn't seen another car all day long, and we would have to stay there until someone came along in a car big enough to give at least some of us a ride to the next town. Water would not be a problem for the next few hours because we carried a large desert water bag on the car radiator, but the sun was beginning to make us sick and dizzy. Dad jacked up the front of the car and we took turns crawling under to get some shade. Late in the afternoon a shadow developed on one side of the car and all of us took refuge there.

Shortly after sundown we saw a car approaching from the east a speck on the horizon, distinguishable at first only as a dust cloud, then as a tiny moving object, and finally, to our joy, as a large truck. The driver surveyed our situation and announced that he was going to Needles, about 125 miles away, but that he would take us to the nearest settlement and order us a new axle when he got to Needles. The settlement, only 20 miles west, had a garage and cafe run by a young couple who treated us as if we were close friends or relatives. He towed our car in from the desert and took us to a near-by camp where we put up our tent. She provided us dinner, as guests. The next day he managed to find a suitable axle from a junk car and on the third day installed it. Just as we were leaving, the new axle arrived from Needles, so we had a spare. We will never forget the kindness shown to us by the good people of the Arizona desert, who could have taken advantage of our helplessness and charged a fortune for their services, but who did just the opposite.

In Needles we learned a strange new fact about life in the desert. A desert town can be hotter than its surrounding area. Needles' air was shimmering as we drove down the main drag. The street and buildings along the way seemed to glow like a well-fired furnace. It was hard to breathe.

Yet, in the midst of this inferno, Tom Mix, the great cowboy movie star, was making another epic. We were stopped by two policemen, who told us the scene then being shot would take another hour to complete and that we might just as well get out and enjoy ourselves. We searched out an ice cream parlor and from the relative cool of its verandah watched Tom ride up to a saloon on his faithful horse Tony, fire a few shots in the air, leap to the ground and tackle the villain as he tried to escape from the building. Bernice and I had never seen a movie, not to mention a movie in the making, so we thought we were seeing the real thing. But Mother and Dad and Frances and Max knew all about Tom Mix, and at the end of the filming they rushed up to shake his hand and get his autograph. Tom, who earned peanuts as a cowboy before he learned that he could make millions doing the same things before a camera, put his sweaty arms around Dad and told him that he too should consider a movie career. Dad figured that he was being kidded, but never forgot the remark. With passing time, he liked to tell his friends that Tom Mix had once invited him to join his company.

What would the average family do today if six relatives moved in on them? Scream, I imagine. But not my Mother's sister, Aunt Nettie Christiansen. When we arrived at her Alameda home, across the bay from San Francisco and just a mile from Oakland, she cried with delight. Though the house was no bigger than most other Alameda residences, it was magically arranged to accommodate all of us with ease. We pitched in to help with the cooking, the shopping, making beds, cleaning up and doing dishes. At night we kids listened to music on the phonograph and played games while our parents talked and talked and talked. We made friends with neighborhood kids. Life was beautiful. Then Dad announced that he had found a job at Battlattes slaughterhouse in Hayward, 10 miles away, and that we would move to the area and live in our tent until we could rent a house. We did not want to leave. We loved it right where we were. But move we did and just a short time later Max discovered that he could knock out a man weighing more than 200 pounds with just one right hand swing. Life would never again be the same for him or any of the rest of us.

WILD WEST ON THE BAY

Only a few traces of it remain today, but when we first came upon the scene the eastern shores and environs of San Francisco Bay were still the Wild West. Livermore, where we moved in 1925, would have needed no props to be the locale of a Hoot Gibson or Tom Mix movie (and in fact the area had been used for movie making a few years earlier, before Los Angeles became the headquarters). Tens of thousands of acres extending from well north of Livermore, south to the fledgling town of San Jose, were rangeland for large cattle herds. Naturally the area was sprinkled with slaughterhouses, which meant that Dad never had a problem finding a job in the several places we lived including Hayward, San Leandro, Galt and Livermore.

It was a 60-mile-long stretch of rolling hills and flatland lapped by the waters of the bay to the west and parched by the scorching summer heat of the San Joaquin Valley to the east. Real cowhands roamed the range in territory that today is better suited for stockbrokers, land developers and urban cowboys. Round-ups, a regular feature of life in those parts was good for business and the sporting life. Cattle auctions, slaughterhouses, meat packing and marketing pumped a lot of money into local economies, and provided the where-with-all for long days and nights of revelry in downtown speakeasies and country roadhouses.

It was, after all, the middle 'twenties'. Times were good. Illicit booze flowed freely. Flapper women with their new bobbed hair-dos and short skirts danced fast two-steps with sweaty ranch hands who stepped all over their new high-heeled shoes in clumsy attempts to go with the new flow. It certainly was not the "West" of San Francisco, just a few miles away, or of Los Angeles 400 miles south. The landscape was unspoiled, the customs open and trusting, the time exciting, and we were lucky to have been there when, one by one, Frances, Max, Bernice and I ended our childhood.

In 1926 Frances turned 21. She had graduated from high school and was working for the Phone Company in Hayward. Soon she would marry, give up her job and raise her own family. The rest of us were in Galt, a small town south of Sacramento in the Great Central Valley. Max, at 17, was on the high school baseball team. In one game he hit a home run ball that wasn't found until the next day. It had carried more than 600 feet into the dark recesses of a fruit packing plant situated just beyond the outer boundary of center field. But in that same game, while playing the outfield, he caught a fly ball on the bridge of his nose. The ball bounced high in the air and was caught by a back-up fielder before it hit the ground. Max's nose was broken, and he carried visible evidence of it the rest of his life.

Galt had a downtown dance hall that was dry and strictly legal. But Galt had another dance hall a few miles out of town that served whatever customers wanted and could pay for. The price, reflecting the risk of arrest or payoff to avoid arrest, was high. Max couldn't afford the tab, but on this particular night he was with some buddies and they all decided that they, too, would like to get in the swing of things. After watching a few dances, they went outside and talked about how they might come up with something more exciting than lemonade.

"See that car over there?" one of the group asked Max, who was looked upon as the leader because of his size and sports abilities. "That belongs to Eddie Overholt. He nearly always keeps a jug of something in there. I know, because he's given me drinks. Maybe I should take a look." Everybody agreed. A few minutes later he returned with a gallon of red wine Portagee poison, they called it and they began to drink.

Half a gallon later they were boisterously boasting about what girls they would dance with before the night ended, when out came Overholt who went straight to his car and reached into the back seat for his bottle. Nothing. Glancing over at Max and his crowd, and seeing his jug being openly passed around, he walked toward them with menacing gait and loud growls.

"Who stole it?" he demanded. "One of you bastards stole my wine'. Raise your hand and I'll kick the shit out of you." The group hurriedly decided that Max should take the rap and they would back him up if need be. Max's hand slowly moved upward. He fluttered his fingers and said in a high falsetto voice, "I did, sir. Please be gentle."

Overholt (as he himself said later) weighed 210 pounds and carried no fat. He was a steeplejack and also wrestled steers, baled hay and built fences for a living. He didn't lock his car because it never occurred to him that anyone would dare touch it. At this moment, his anger over the theft had turned into rage at being made the butt of Max's humor, and he rushed into battle.

Max adroitly back-stepped when Overholt swung with his right, causing him to lose his balance. Before he could recoup Max knocked him to the ground with a left. He jumped up and whistled a left-right combination to Max's head, connecting with the latter, but Max shook it off, laughed, and crashed his right squarely on Overholt's nose and mouth. It was all over for Overholt, who lay quivering on his back. Max bent down to ask if he was alright, then helped him to his feet and braced him until he could stand without staggering. Overholt put out his hand and said shakily, "you didn't really steal my bottle, did you?" Max said he hadn't, but added that he had agreed that someone else do it, "Well, you win anyhow, and Christ, I swear I have never been hit like that by anyone or anything. You ought to go into boxing." Then Overholt offered to drive Max home. Max accepted, and they became friends for years to come.

Until then, Max had never given a fleeting thought to the idea of boxing, either for fun or profit. But Overholt's words echoed in his head, and the echo didn't fade. Rather, it persisted and grew stronger as people he had never met came up to congratulate him on his win. He enjoyed the notoriety, the more so because he had not realized the extent to which Overholt was esteemed both as a fighter and as a man, and also because Overholt himself was spreading the word that he had a killer punch. It was heady stuff for Max, who just two years earlier had thought of himself as a coward.

When we moved back to Livermore the next year, and Dad leased acreage for a hog farm, Max dropped out of school. For a while he helped out on the farm, then got his first job at a nearby gravel pit. The strenuous labor in the pit seemed to hasten what nature was doing naturally making him into a spectacular physical Specimen. He was over six feet tall and growing. His torso plunged from shoulders 56 inches wide to a 32-inch waist. His legs were strong, long and well developed. Women noticed him admiringly, and finally he was becoming aware of this pleasant state of affairs. To show his appreciation of their appreciation, he once allowed two giggling teenagers to sit on his shoulders, one on each side, and pranced around in a circle as they laughed and screamed to be let down, and when he let them down, clamored to be picked up again. Max Baer was beginning to like himself.

Livermore had a gymnasium. Max started going there, steered by Overholt's echo. The place had four walls, a set of parallel bars and not much else. Would-be boxers brought their own equipment. So Max, after several paydays at the pit, invested in a punching bag, boxing gloves and trunks. He slapped amateurishly at the bag, but with enough force to attract the attention of Percy Madsen, a local boxing instructor. Mr. Madsen agreed to teach Max what he knew about the sport, and from that time forward Max knew what he wanted to do with his life.

The West wasn't as wild for me, mainly because, at age 12, I was interested in things that were associated more with the East than the West. Like art and singing. I started drawing about this time and found, to my delight, that even without instruction I was able to make a moon that looked like the moon. If you should think it's easy, try it. Then I did faces. Surprisingly, boys looked like boys, girls like girls, men like men. At first, I copied from pictures, but soon was drawing from my imagination. My parents noticed, approvingly, but didn't suggest that I might have artistic ability worth developing. So I just doodled away on my own as I continued to grow up.

And grow I did. At age 15 I passed the six-foot mark. When I started riding streetcars to school, conductors viewed me suspiciously. How could anyone so big be a student? (Student fares were only 5 cents, half the regular fare.) Initially I was embarrassed, but they got to know me and the suspicion that I was a cheapskate adult faded away.

I was as shy as I was big for my age. I don't know what caused it, because I was always happy. Mother continued to call me her "baby, and I liked it. But she put the same discipline on me that she had used with Max, Bernice and Frances, so I was in no way spoiled. Maybe my shyness came from the exceptional happiness I had at home, where life was complete and I didn't really need other people. But that was true for all of us. We loved our parents as much as they loved us, and later as we went our own ways in life they remained as close as ever before.

The hog ranch was a big success. Dad at one time had more than 2,400 of the creatures around. The market was good and we prospered. He bought a Lincoln sedan a prestige car at the time, which Max learned to drive, and which may explain his life-long taste for the best in automotive equipment. Dad taught Max, but I learned to drive on my own, chugging around the circular driveway in front of our ranch house, at the wheel of the ranch truck. To refresh my memory for this story I recently visited the ranch house, a portion of which is still there as part of a vastly improved home. It's still called "Twin Oaks." Time has not erased the beauty of the site, which overlooks a bucolic valley of small farms and rangeland nestled between brown hills dotted with green Oak trees and a scattering of Eucalyptus. The sight assured me that my fond memories were based on facts, not nostalgia.

I remember that our house, wherever we were, was always open to strangers, drifters who arrived by foot, by freight train or by courtesy of drivers who picked them up on the road. They stopped at our place because they had heard, through the magical grapevine that passed such information to the wandering homeless, that the Baer family was always good for a meal. It was true, though Mother or Dad would ask them to work for it if there were any chores around that needed to be done. On the ranch, they chopped firewood, but in town, more often than not, there wasn't any appropriate work and they were fed simply for the asking. If we had old clothing in excess, and they needed it, they were given it. On the ranch, where we had a barn, they were permitted to spend the night, using blankets and bedding that we provided. In those days, we didn't think of possible harm or theft by the hands of any of these passing strangers, for crime as we know it today did not exist. Instead, they gave us their gratitude.

Mother's and Dad's compassion for people less fortunate than they led directly to a kind of adoption that would not be legally possible today. When we were living in Hayward, we frequently heard the sounds and cries of a child being whipped in the house directly behind ours. The child was Augie Silva, youngest of a large family, and it seemed that he could do no right. He was severely beaten by his stepfather for minor conduct infractions, some of which were imagined. For example, he came home from school early one day, saying that classes had been dismissed. His stepfather beat him that night for playing hooky and lying about it. But he hadn't lied. School really had closed early. He was forced to work every night until midnight, using a machete to slowly dig out space for a cellar under the house. He worked in cramped space no more than three feet high for months on end. Mother and Dad were concerned about his survival and invited him to come live with us.

Augie moved in, and his sister and brother-in-law objected. Dad said, "go tell your story to the police, and I'll tell them mine." The Silvas declined to go that far, and so it was that Augie became a member of our family. In fact, he was the last of us kids to leave home, and to this day is just as close to me as my sisters and we to him. He changed his name to Baer in his early 'twenties.

All of our chores at the ranch were not bodybuilding or backbreaking. Every day Max and I were assigned the duty of picking up two-day-old cookies at Mother's Cookie Factory in East Oakland, which would have thrown them out if we hadn't volunteered to take them. We hauled them away by the truckload. We ate some, but the purpose of it all was to add a delicious dimension to our hogs' diet. Dad maintained jokingly that we had the "most delicate hogs in the country, they have dessert with their meals." Sometimes he included Max and me in his description.

It was while we were on the hog ranch that I discovered I could sing well enough to carry a tune that others recognized. So I sang while I did my chores, sang while I walked across the countryside, sang when I picked cherries to make a little extra money, sang when I stood in the outfield waiting for a ball to come my way as I played for the local baseball team, and of course, I sang in the bathroom. Mr. Gardella, one of the more prominent people in Livermore, heard me singing on the sidewalk and asked me to render "0 So Oh Mio." Which I did, having learned it from a phonograph record. He offered to send me to Italy on a voice scholarship. Mother was pleased, but Dad said my voice was good enough for hog calling and not much else. As time passed, I forgot about it, and considering the exciting life that lay ahead, it probably was for the best.

I could have been an artist, maybe. I could have been an opera singer, perhaps. And possibly I could have been a professional baseball player, so I was told by school coaches and other baseball people in Livermore. They said I could hit farther than Max, and run, field and throw with the best in town. I'll never know how good I might have been at football, because Mother laid down the law. "You can't play, it's too dangerous," she said. Football coaches looked at my size and speed and cried. They tried to persuade Mother, to no avail. Mom was tough when she considered the issue important. So I was saved for the prize ring.

MAX UNTAMED

Max was 18 when his encounter with Overholt gave him the idea that he could make a living knocking professional fighters on their duffs. Actually, his entire personality was changing from shyness and quiet introspection to outgoing friendliness and confidence in himself. His work on the ranch amazed Dad, who had noticed that Max outperformed seasoned hands in anything he did, from slugging a 1,200-pound bull with a deadly single blow of an axe, to digging post holes for fencing, pounding in the posts, stringing the wire taut, or plowing, or felling trees and removing stumps. Max was very strong, and he had endurance. Dad told him many times how good he was, and his words did much to boost his self-confidence. It was the same story at the gravel pit, where old timers wondered at his strength, enthusiasm and unflagging toil. Two quick pay raises of 10 cents an hour did nothing to dispel his developing attitude that life was easy, uncomplicated and rosy. After Overholt, it was natural that he would figure boxing was just as easy as anything else he had done. All you had to do was slug the other guy and he would collapse for the count.

He actually started a fight with a cowboy who he said had insulted him, something about his being afraid of girls, because he never had dates. Instead of laughing it off in his normal manner, he challenged him to fight and rushed him with a flurry of wild swings, one of which landed and knocked him cold. That was not Max's style, then or ever after, but it did reveal his new found curiosity about himself as a fighter, and the continuing growth of his confidence that he could excel at whatever he wanted to do. Years later he said that he was not proud of himself for starting the cowboy fight. It weighed on his conscience as an unjustified attack on a man he knew he could beat, but it taught him never to needlessly display his fighting prowess. And from that day forward, he never did.

Percy Madsen was Livermore's reigning expert on boxing, having flirted with a career in the art but settling for a peripheral relationship as a part-time trainer of local hopefuls. Visiting the Livermore gym one evening he heard Max before he saw him. He followed the sound to a far corner of the noisy room where Max was producing a drumbeat of thunder that rose above the general din. "I was awed at the power he used in attacking his punching bag," Madsen told a San Francisco sports writer several years later. "I thought the bag might fly apart, a KO of an inanimate object."

On return trips to the gym he watched Max spar with whoever was around. Maybe "spar" is not the right word, for Max made no attempt to box. He simply attacked, and while he invariably sent his opponent sprawling, he was just as invariably wide open to a counter-attack by anyone having minimum skills. Madsen told Max that he had the power to win in boxing, but he needed to develop a defense, a variety of punches, footwork, and a sense of strategy in approaching an opponent. When he suggested that Max go into serious training under the guidance of a real professional, Max readily agreed. Madsen then arranged for Max to work with Ray Pelkey, a former middleweight who presided over training at the Yosemite Gym in Oakland.

So Max moved away from home for the first time, finding a job in the spare parts department of J. Hamilton Lorimer's Atlas Diesel Engine Company in East Oakland. In his first session with Pelkey, Max tried to impress, and did. He thrust out his chin and asked Ray to hit it. Ray socked it with authority several times, and each time Max laughed and said, "try again." Clearly, he could take it, but Pelkey tried without much success to convince Max that taking it was only part of the game. "The main idea is to keep from being hit, and to hit the other guy," he pleaded. "To avoid punches you must be able to dance, duck and jab. It's what we call boxing. Have you ever heard of it?"

Max heard but didn't hear. In every sparring session he waded into his opponent with roundhouse rights and uppercuts, speedily flattening him. His supply of sparring partners quickly dried up. They said they wanted to learn boxing, not slugging, and anyhow they didn't appreciate being knocked cold while trying to learn. Pelkey was getting nowhere with his 18 year-old strong boy.

Max was making an impression in his place of employment as well as in the Yosemite Gym. As usual, he was good at his job. He had learned automobile mechanics at home, tearing down his own car and friends' cars and putting them back together. He knew the function of every part, and at the diesel plant he proved an apt learner in the business side of parts inventory, ordering, estimating demand, and quality control. J. Hamilton Lorimer, son of the owner, considered him an up and coming addition to the work force. But "Ham," as he was known to his friends, also loved boxing, and since he knew that Max was training downtown he invited him to use the factory basement for his workouts. Max gladly accepted, and proceeded to maltreat a series of one-time-only volunteer sparring mates who also worked at the plant.

Soon Ham did a strange thing he signed Max to a three-year contract as his fighter, good until Max reached his 21st birthday. I say "strange" because Ham did not want Max to give up his promising career in the Diesel Company to become a fighter. He thought Max was unteachable in the finer points of boxing, and therefore would be mangled by good professionals. He later explained his contradictory behavior (again to a San Francisco sports reporter) as due to his belief that Max would be beaten in his first fight or two and give up his illusion that he could succeed in a sport where 19 out of 20 failed.

Ham set about proving his thesis by arranging to fight with a tough Indian heavyweight, Chief

Cariboo, in Stockton's Oak Park arena. Cariboo was considered an excellent club fighter and was very popular with the fans. He definitely was not the type of fighter the average manager would choose as an opponent for his man's first outing. Ham thought the chief would give Max the beating of his life, and contribute to an early decision by Max that the ring was not for him, after all. It very nearly turned out that way.

Max knew almost nothing about how to train for a fight, not because Pelkey hadn't tried to teach him, but because he wouldn't listen. One hour before the Cariboo brawl, Max, feeling a powerful thirst, drank several bottles of a carbonated soft drink. Pelkey was aghast when he learned about it, but there was nothing to be done at that late hour to remove the gas from his stomach except what the chief might do. At the sound of the bell Max rushed out to meet Cariboo, swinging wildly as he got within range. The chief side stepped and Max stumbled into the ropes. Back came Max with a flying haymaker that missed by two feet. Cariboo shot a stiff left into Max's stomach. Max gasped with gaseous pain, though the punch would have doubled up many fighters, and responded with a clumsy right that accidentally clipped the chief's head with his elbow, sending him down for a count of two. Max pursued Cariboo around the ring, missing four or five punches to land one, and taking repeated blows to the midriff. Nausea swept over him. An overhand right by Max nailed the chief on his chin, and down he went for the second time. Bouncing back, the chief assaulted Max's body, for he could plainly see Max was unusually sensitive in that area. Max turned green, but valiantly fought on, never thinking that he might throw some body punches himself, always aiming for the chin, missing most of the time, and finally connecting with another wallop that decked Cariboo for the third time just before the bell.

When the second round began Max was deathly sick and his arms felt almost too heavy to lift. Even so, he came out of his corner with marvelously simulated verve and pep, only to run into another barrage of body blows. Cariboo had diagnosed his man, and found him wanting in the belly. He paid a price, however, as Max floored him with a left hand smash to his jaw. To Max's dismay, Cariboo rose again and slowly advanced. Max knew that he would be finished himself if he did not now finish off the chief. He summoned all of his fading strength and in a final, desperate effort found Cariboo's chin with a right uppercut that laid the Indian low for several times the 10-count. He had won his first ring battle. He had surmounted the heavy handicap of lousy training that he had imposed upon himself. And he had, through his own courage and lethal power, poked a gaping hole in Lorimer's plan for his future.

Lorimer, however, was only partially convinced that he might indeed have a consistent winner on his hands. He promptly signed Max to fight a rugged, rarely defeated knockout specialist by the name of Sailor Leeds. Leeds, without question, was the toughest fighter Lorimer could get in

Northern California to face his novice wild man. His record included a string of first round punchouts and he was highly regarded for his ability to absorb punishment. He would, Lorimer thought, be more than a match for Max. The fight, also staged in Stockton, ended in less than two minutes. Max, who had dieted properly for this engagement, hit the sailor with a whirlwind of punches thrown from downtown Oakland and the suburbs of nearby Sacramento. Leeds fell and rose twice before crashing stiffly to the canvas like a falling tree. Lorimer stared incredulously as the crowd cheered, sensing the presence of an important new name in boxing.

Lorimer felt it too. He decided it was time to move Max into a top-level training routine under a nationally recognized trainer, Bob McAllister. McAllister had been a classy enough middleweight to be compared for style with Jim Corbett, but he was waylaid along the championship road by the St. Paul Phantom, Mike Gibbons, and thereafter earned a comfortable living in insurance and teaching boxing to others. In the meantime, Lorimer made a highly tangible expression of his confidence in Max by giving him a $3,800 Cord convertible, perhaps the most prestigious and certainly the most exciting car in America. Max, the epitome of flaming youth, knew what to do with his prize, and for the first time in my memory he was to be seen careening through downtown Oakland streets and flashing over country roads with a. girl at his side.

Love came late, but lustily, for my dear brother. For some time he had been the object of admiring stares from many lovely young ladies, which he didn't return, probably because he simply did not realize he was being noticed. Now it was different. He was a mini-celebrity in Oakland and Stockton, though his slightly elevated status was limited to the sports fans of both cities. His name had appeared in San Francisco press accounts of club fights in the area, and one reporter had called his right hand "murderous." But in those days there were many clubs and many fighters, Max being only one who was receiving favorable comment. Anyhow, I'm sure that Max's small reputation as a fighter, after only two bouts, was just the icing on the cake in the eyes of his female admirers. The male animal himself was the main attraction, and his Cord convertible didn't hurt his image a bit.

It came to pass, then, in the year 1929, when he was not yet 19, that Max Baer took unto his bosom his first steady girl friend, one Olive Beck, who worked as a waitress in a Livermore coffee shop, Molly's Grill. I met her and thought her both beautiful and fascinating, even though I still was not old enough to fully appreciate feminine charms. Her voice had a musical lilt that appealed to me very much. She laughed a lot. She smiled easily and naturally. She looked at Max in a way that would have melted the polar ice cap, but that buffoon would respond with the latest joke he had picked up at the gym, guffaw loudly at his own humor, pat her on the head and drive off in a swirl of dust to show her what the Cord could do in high on a hill.

Later on, after Max had achieved national prominence, both as a fighter and a lover, Olive sued Max for breach of promise. I have never known what promises, if any, Max made to Olive, but I do know that they reached a financial settlement that was satisfactory to both. I also know that Max was very generous and that he didn't like arguments.

Max had many girl friends. He was literally surrounded by women, who lured him into chasing them to bed, yet another sport in which he excelled. For adventurous women, Max had it all brawn, personality, a sunny disposition, a flashy car, growing fame, and money. He received $35 for the Cariboo fight, $50 for knocking Leeds senseless, small change today, but at a time when prices were low, income taxes unheard of for the average man, and the dollar worth a dollar, Max thought he had struck the Mother Lode. You could make a big splash at the soda fountain with 50 cents.

In 1929 Max had a total of 27 fights in Oakland, Stockton and San Francisco. From the third or fourth fight on he was the most popular club fighter north of Los Angeles, and his purses proved it. He earned $50,000 before the year was over. Many top name, ranked fighters were not doing nearly so well financially.

In addition to Cariboo and Leeds, Max cold-cocked Tillie Taverna twice, in the first and second rounds; Al Ledford twice, both in the second round; George Van Schultz and Frank Budjenski in the fourth; George Carroll, Alec Rowe and Tony Fuente in the first; Chet Shandell in the second, and Cariboo again, in the first. He won decisions over Benny Hill twice and Natie Brown once. The big shock of the year for Max was an August 3 loss to Jack McCarthy, on a foul. He didn't intend to hit low, of course, but his flamboyant ring behavior carried with it a high risk that one of his lumberjack swings would land in foul territory. The McCarthy fight was only Max's sixth. He was just a beginner. But he didn't learn from the experience. He fought his 27th fight that year without having ever attempted to jab, weave or deceive. Slugging worked for him. Most fighters now feared his right, and fought so cautiously that he could crash through their defenses with sheer power. McAllister kept telling him that he could not reach the big time until he mastered at least a few of the basic techniques of boxing. "Sure, sure," Max would say. "What's the point of the fancy stuff? It just wastes time. I'll catch the dancers sooner or later, and they'll go down."

The dawn of 1930 found Max $10,000 in debt, which worried him no more than owing the grocer $5. In spending $50,000 he acquired two more fancy cars, one of which he gave to Mother and Dad, and a reputation as "Madcap Maxie," "the Larruping Lothario of Livermore," and the "Squire of Dames." But he soon was to learn that silver clouds can suddenly darken and chill one's soul.

BANNED IN CALIFORNIA

The stock market had crashed the previous October, and judging by what we read in the papers some of the bloom was off the economic rose back east. But here in California the affects had not been felt, and the roaring 'twenties' slipped easily into January, 1930, the month that Max lost his second fight, again on a foul, again because of his wild swinging, this time in the third round to a lumbering heavyweight by the name of Tiny Abbott. McAllister threatened Max that he would quit and stop worrying about him if he didn't tone down his fighting style and pay more attention to boxing as a craft. "I'll show Abbott that I can box and still beat him," Max responded. "Tell Ham to get me a return engagement." Ham did, and two weeks later Max knocked Abbott out in the sixth round without throwing a single jab or sidestepping a single Abbott punch.

"I think the reason you guys don't like my style is because I'm not messed up in the face," Max told Ham and McAllister. "So I don't have a cauliflower ear. Would you be happy if I got a cauliflower ear?" Without waiting for an answer he walked over to a steam radiator in the gym and banged the side of his head repeatedly against the metal. When his ear bled he returned proudly to his astounded critics and proclaimed, "Now that I've got what you want, lay off and let me fight my way."

After disposing of Jack Stewart in two rounds at the Oakland Auditorium, a cavernous arena by comparison with the Arcadia Pavilion where many of his other fights had been held, and filling the place to capacity-plus, Max was ready to make his Los Angeles debut. The fight against Ernie Owens, which he won in ten by decision, was of secondary importance to the L.A. fight crowd. They adored everything about Max, starting with his spectacular arrival at the auditorium for a contract signing ceremony a few days before the fight. He pulled up in front of the building in a chauffeur-driven limousine, stepped out with the aid of a footman, and bowed deeply to scattered cameramen, dressed in boots and togs designed for riding to hounds. When the laughter and applause from the small crowd died down, he predicted a terrible fate for Mr. Owens, flashed the winning smile that appeared on page 1 of all sports sections the next day, and mugged his way to celebrity before a blow had been struck in the much ballyhooed fight. Of course, his reputation had preceded him. Fans only hoped that he would live up to that reputation and he certainly did.

One of Max's fans was the comedy and singing star, Al Jolson, who had seen Max perform in San Francisco. Al was so impressed with Max that he brought fight promoter Ancil Hoffman with him to see the Owens match. Hoffman was a wealthy avocado grower from Sacramento who then was spending most of his time, and some of his money, in trying to produce a boxing champion. Max chased Owens all over the ring for 10 rounds, turning the smoky air into gusty drafts with thunderous swings that missed their target. But, miracle of miracles, he threw enough straight lefts and two-handed jabs to pile up a winning point total. The fans and the press, far from being disappointed, loved his aggressive style. More importantly, Hoffman was impressed, and made his initial move to buy up as much of Max's contract as he could get. Which wasn't much, because Lorimer wished to retain control.

Having firmly established the Baer presence in the consciousness of Los Angelenos, who had a special talent for recognizing theatrical material when they saw it, Max moved his boxing show

From the very beginning of his career, Max always drew a crowd at the training sessions, promoted by methods as unrefined as his boxing style. This probably dates from 1930, in California.

back to Oakland and a series of five sell-outs at the auditorium. He flattened Tom Toner in six on May 7, scored first-round kayo's over.

Jack Linkhorn and Buck Weaver on May 28 and June 11, and on June 25 he finally caught up with Owens in a return match and knocked him out in the fifth. So it was back to L.A. to capitalize on those victories, but this time, on July 15, his untamed points, he fouled Les Kennedy in the 10th and lost. But the fans declared him the winner in spirit, noisily booing the unfortunate Kennedy and cheering Max as he walked spiritedly back to his dressing room. Max never let defeat get in the way of his fun. He waved and blew kisses to the admiring throng just as if he had won. Afterward, he told reporters, between jokes and hammy poses for the photographers, that even though the fight had been taken away from him he learned enough from his mistakes to carry him all the way to the top.

Ancil Hoffman thought it was time for Max to be tested by the only heavyweight on the Pacific coast, other than his own fighter, who seemed to be poised for a leap into national pugilistic stardom. Frankie Campbell, a native of Dinuba in the San Joaquin Valley, had won a large following of fans with a series of colorful victories in Los Angeles and San Franciso.

He was an expert at playing possum. When hit with a reasonably respectable punch, he would stagger, seem confused and cover up. Invariably, his opponent would rush in for the kill, leaving himself wide open in his anxiety to administer the coup de grace. Suddenly Campbell would lash out furiously and reverse the situation, frequently knocking out his surprised victim.

Ham Lorimer, who still had controlling interest in Max, agreed with Hoffman that they should try to arrange a match with Campbell. They reached an agreement with Carol Working, Campbell's manager, to hold the fight on August 25 in Recreation Park, home of the San Francisco Seals baseball club. The aging park, built in 1907, was already scheduled for demolition the next year when the baseballers would move to a grand new Seals stadium. But it was located in a relatively fog-free section of the city's Mission District called the "Banana Belt, and would be ideal for a 10 p.m. main event.

A capacity crowd of nearly 20 000 filled the creaking structure when Max and Frankie answered the bell for Round One. Both fighters had done their homework on each other's strengths and weaknesses, so Frankie had great respect for Max's right, and Max was determined not to be fooled by Frankie's favorite ruse. Frankie jolted Max with a right-left combination to the chin, eluded Max's counter punching, moved inside and peppered Max's ribs with short, stinging blows. As he stepped back Max caught him on the chin with his left, sending him to the canvas for a count of nine. For the rest of the round he stayed out of range, and Max couldn't catch him.

In Round Two Max missed with a sweeping right that threw him slightly off balance. Before he could recover Frankie grazed his chin with a whistling left, and Max slipped to the deck. Frankie, thinking he had scored a knockdown, sauntered toward his corner but unexplainably stopped short and looked out over the ropes at the crowd. Referee Toby Irwin ruled that Max had slipped, and motioned him back into action. As the daydreaming Campbell turned back to the ring, Max was upon him and loosed a vicious blow to the side of his head. Max said later that a photographer's flash bulb went off just as he reached Campbell, and that he saw only a blurred vision of Campbell when he threw his punch. Anyway, Frankie managed to hold on until the round ended, when he was heard to tell his handlers, "I felt something snap in my head."

Frankie showed little evidence of the blow in the next two rounds, in which he rolled up a point advantage with quick stabs to Max's face and body, all the while retreating before Max's steady pursuit. Max found his solar plexus with a solid left toward the end of the fourth round, and at the bell sensed that Frankie was weakening.

Early in the fifth Max scored with two powerful rights to the head. Frankie reeled into the ropes. Max, suspicious that this might be the possum game, approached carefully and aimed another right to Frankie's jaw. He sagged into the middle strand of rope and sat on it, held upright by the upper strand. The referee stood by without giving any kind of signal, so Max struck again with a flurry of punches that swayed Frankie's body from side to side. Max thought he was weaving to protect himself, and therefore still fighting. Then Frankie slumped to the canvas, the referee pushed Max away and raised his hand in victory. At no time did Frankie's head hit any part of the ringpost, as the press reported and as has since become part of the legend of that terrible fight.

After Max had showered he asked Ancil whether he should visit Frankie in his dressing room and wish him well. He was shocked to learn that Frankie was still in the ring and had not regained consciousness. Some 30 minutes after the fight ended an ambulance arrived from Mission Emergency Hospital, and Max went home to nervously await news of Frankie's condition. A phone call the next morning provided the worst news possible. Frankie had died of a cerebral hemorrhage.

Max was emotionally demolished. He cried uncontrollably for hours. Mother and Dad tried to comfort him, explaining that this tragedy could have befallen any fighter, but it was no use. Still weeping, Max visited Frankie's widow at the hospital, and she, in much worse condition than Max, found it in herself to put her arms around him and say, "it could just as easily have been you who died."

Max was arrested and jailed that afternoon, charged with manslaughter. Bail was set at $10,000, a new high in San Francisco for that charge. He stayed in jail until nightfall when Ancil obtained release of Max's share of the fight purse, which coincidentally equaled the bail amount, and turned it over to the court.

The charge of manslaughter was legally indefensible and the court so found in dismissing it after a hearing at which it was shown that boxing was legal and that Max operated within the rules of the sport. Both fighters had been admonished before the bout by the California Boxing Commission to fight as long as the other was standing and the referee had not intervened. Max did only what he was required to do, though he could never have guessed in his wildest imagining that it would lead to so tragic a result.

But clearance by the court was not clearance by the public, especially the press. Sportswriter Harry B. Smith of the San Francisco <u>Chronicle</u> seemed to suggest that Max knew when he was pounding Campbell into unconsciousness that he was wreaking great harm upon him. "He was ready to drop," Smith reported, "but Baer continued to rain in blows to an unprotected jaw and against a man who was already knocked out ... Campbell was dead to the world and stayed in that unconscious condition as Irwin raised Baer's hand and posed for the picture of the winner." I think, and certainly hope, that Smith later changed his mind about Max, who had no meanness or cruelty in him, then or later.

The loudest criticism of Max came from the San Francisco <u>Examiner,</u> which two years earlier had conducted an unsuccessful campaign to ban boxing in California. But it wasn't only Max who provided the justification for the paper's screaming front-page editorials against "legalized prize ring butchery." A week prior to the Campbell fight an 18-year-old boxer, Johnny Anderson, had died from injuries in a fight with Reinhart Ruehl in San Francisco's National Hall. Most of the <u>Examiner's</u>

fury, however, was directed against Max. I know, as few others alive today know, that Max suffered the tortures of hell in his remorse over Campbell's death. He paid little attention to what the newspapers said. Even if they had been more understanding of his situation, his private agony would not have been eased. He never really recovered from the pain of that time. Not ever.

Lorimer and Hoffman thought they had lost their fighter, the <u>Oakland</u> <u>Tribune</u> published his statement to Ham: "If this is the fight game, I want no more of it. I'd be happier back in the Livermore hills tending pigs. I'm sorry I ever drew on a glove. I'm through, Ham, through with the racket forever. I could never forget what I've gone through since poor Frankie went down in that fifth round." Ham did his best, along with Hoffman, to assure him that it was an accident, that it wasn't his fault. My brother was not consoled.

The boxing commission, the very same men who warned Max and Campbell to keep fighting as long as the other was on his feet sanctimoniously found all parties to the fight in violation of something, and suspended them for a year. It was never made clear on what grounds the commission issued its ban. Campbell's manager and his seconds, Max's seconds and Ham and Ancil, along with the referee, were affected by the decision. In my own mind only two of the group really merited punishment, the referee, who should have stopped the fight as soon as Campbell fell on the ropes, and Campbell's manager, who should have thrown in the towel. The guiltiest party of all was the commission itself, which steadfastly enforced rules that inevitably would lead to tragedy, and which it refused to change after tragedy had struck. But there was some balm for Max in what the commission did. He didn't want to fight anymore, anyway.

HELLO BROADWAY

The two months following Campbell's funeral were unpleasant for everyone in the Baer family and our circle of friends. Max moped through the days, saying little and eating less. I felt his depression and behaved sympathetically, almost as if I were part of his psyche. He lost weight. Ancil and Ham groused that he was endangering not only his career but also his health, and urged him to eat properly and get some exercise. But Max spent day after day lounging around our house, falling into chair after chair with spring-breaking thuds, pacing from room to room, staring blankly at whatever or whoever was in his field of vision. Mother and Dad let him alone. "He'll snap out of it, if for no other reason than he can't go on like this," I was told.

The turning point came one day in late October when Ham dropped in for a visit and told Max that he was learning something about some people in the fight game that he didn't like. "They are nothing more than ghouls, Max," he said. "I've had many calls from these creeps. They want to buy our contract for about a nickel on the dollar. They think that I think you're washed up and would be willing to sell for virtually nothing. And they think you are so down and out that you wouldn't care." I was there, sitting quietly in the corner, and saw Max bristle. "I would, but you wouldn't, would you?" Max asked, rising and standing tall for the first time in weeks. "Wouldn't what?" Ham responded, looking up at my brother. "I would care a hell of a lot about my contract being traded to a god-damned ghoul, and I hope you feel the same way about it." "I do, and I wouldn't, even if you told me you didn't give a damn," Ham said very slowly. With that he got up, went to the door, opened it, turned to Max and said, "I have confidence in you and your future." Ancil has confidence in you and your future. When you feel like it, get in touch with Ancil. He has an idea that can get us moving again." Then he left.

For the next hour Max stormed through the house, from wall to wall in every room, his voice rising from low mutters to loud shouts, directed at no one and yet everyone. We heard "so they think I'm through," "I'll show them," and "what do they take me for?" He was definitely coming back to the land of the living. That evening he called Ancil.

What Ancil had to say was far better therapy than Max had been imposing on himself though I'm sure both were necessary. If Max hadn't suffered through his private hell, Ancil's proposal would have had no effect. As it was, when Ancil suggested it was time to fight again, and that since California wouldn't let him fight here, why not go to New York, Max reacted as though he had been injected with a double dose of joy juice. He put down the phone and announced, " Mater and Pater, dear sisters and Brother Buddy, you are looking at the next world champion." We cheered and clapped. Dad slapped him on the back and said, "Go get 'em, Maxie. Mom shed a tear. Bernice and Frances, who, like Max, had their own apartments but chose to spend much of their time with Mother and Dad during this period, kissed him.

Several things needed to be settled before New York could become a reality. First, Max was in debt to countless creditors who had sued for payment. Not only did he owe the jeweler, the haberdasher and nightclubs galore; he also was in hock to people who had bought part of him. The latter group accounted for 20 percent of his purses when they could get it. Max described the first sale of himself in a newspaper article written in 1934:

"My pals, the Jacklich brothers in Oakland, thought early in 1930 that I was as good as I had been telling them, and they offered me $15,000 for 10 percent interest. After I had recovered from my dizzy spell, I whispered, 'in cash?' 'Yes.' I signed the papers."

The $15,000 lasted Max just one month, but the Jacklich boys had a lifetime hold on a good slice of Max's ring earnings. Later, he sold another 10 percent of himself to various and sundry investors, leaving only 30 percent for himself (Ham and Ancil evenly divided the remaining 50 percent). With generous help from Ancil, Max was able to satisfy his most demanding creditors and legally clear himself of claims that would prevent him from leaving the state.

Max also was late in making payments on the palatial house he had bought for our parents in the most elite area of Oakland Piedmont, where the smallest structure was a mini-mansion. Mother and Dad never really felt comfortable there, for it was much too big and plush for their needs and style of living. They felt most uncomfortable when they were informed that the monthly payment was overdue. Being retired and on a modest income themselves, there was nothing they could do but squirm and tell Max, who always came through in the end with the necessary green stuff.

And then there were lawsuits over Max's fights. One sought to bar him from the ring because of the Campbell fight. It was brought by Reverend Leslie Kelly, a member of the California Boxing Commission. Max counter-sued Kelly and the matter was settled out of court, with Max regaining his right to fight. Another accused August R. "Gus" Oliva, a San Francisco politician, of bribing Max with an expensive car to "carry" Tiny Abbott for at least four rounds in their second fight. The case died when Ham produced the sales slip for the car he had bought for Max long before the Abbott encounter.

Most important of the obstacles to getting out of state was having a reason to do so. Early in November Ancil took care of that. After nearly two weeks of dickering with Madison Square Garden he was offered a match with Ernie Schaaf, for December 19, 1930. Max's reaction, as explained to the press: "Boys, I did 12 flip-flops! New York! Madison Square Garden! Dorothy!"

Dorothy? He met her in Reno, where she was spending the legally required six weeks to divorce her fourth or fifth husband. Dorothy Dunbar was a New York Socialite and a former movie star. Financially independent and a raving beauty. Max first saw her sitting alone at a casino table. Quicker than the speed of sound he moved to her side and introduced himself. If she had ever heard of him she used her acting ability well to feign ignorance and worse, indifference. Without the trace of a smile she said, "so what?" and blew a long trail of cigarette smoke toward the ceiling. Max was overcome. He remembered it this way:

"I can't remember if I proposed the first minute, or whether it was formal and I waited five minutes. Was I in love! Boys, I was on fire like a volcano, and had just one thought in life, to marry Dorothy.' She was poised, older by at least 10 years, and her response to Max's overture was to treat him as a child still wet behind his ears. "Have you started to earn your own living, yet?" she asked. I need not go into details of Max's reply, but he did give her a glowing account of his accomplishments. She remained unimpressed. "Was I wounded," Max said later. "I was ready to forget all about being a fighter, but her indifference stirred me up." I have no doubt that most of the $15,000 Max received from the Jacklich brothers was spent in Reno, trying to impress upon Dorothy that he was already a man of the world.

Dorothy got her divorce and returned to New York, but not before telling Max that if he wanted to see her again he had better brush up on his manners, his speech and his dress. "You're cute, but so are the apes at Central Park Zoo," as she delicately put it. Max couldn't be insulted, and promised that when she saw him again she would think he had been appointed to an ambassador's post.

Unfortunately for Max, when Ancil told him they would leave for New York in one week, his money was gone. How to acquire the wardrobe he thought would impress Dorothy? His 1929 Cord was too old, so how to equip himself with the latest and best from Detroit? Without consulting Ancil, he ordered 12 suits from Oakland's most expensive tailor, persuading the tailor to wait for payment until he won the championship, which he said was a "cinch." Ancil even went so far as to tell the tailor that it would be a bargain for him if he were to give Max the suits, because he could then advertise that he had supplied "The great Max Baer, Heavyweight Champion of the World," with his entire wardrobe. He performed the same miracle with the Cadillac dealer, who gladly gave him credit for a 16-cylinder town limousine, to be delivered on his arrival in New York. To top everything off, he convinced his chauffeur, Alden Humphries, to assume the added duties of personal secretary and accompany him to the Big Town all on a promise to pay later. "Financing yourself isn't tough if you just learn how," Max said.

Off they went to the city of San Francisco, New York bound. The traveling party included Ancil and Mrs. Hoffman, trainer Frankie Burns and Mrs. Burns, Max, his secretary-chauffeur Alden Humphries, and six trunks belonging to Max ("filled," he boasted, "with more goodies than Beau Brummel could use."). Ham did not go, for he had become so enmeshed in his own business that he agreed to gradually turn over his share of the contract to Ancil for a price.

Ernie Schaaf was ranked in the top five of the world's heavyweights. Along with Tommy Loughran he was considered one of the two best boxers in the division. Unlike Loughran, who wore his victims down, Ernie packed a knockout punch. Max should have been worried, for never in his career had he been scheduled to step in the same ring with such a man. He should have been worried enough to hit the road every morning for miles of running to toughen his legs and extend his physical endurance. He should have sparred seriously and long with his stable of paid punchers. He should have cut out the booze, the cigarettes, and food he didn't need. Not our Maxie.

"Don't worry about this bum Schaaf," he told Ancil. "I'll knock him stiff like I did the others.

"With a baseball bat, maybe," Ancil replied. "You're stepping into the big league now. You know a little bit more about defense than you did a year ago and every once in awhile I think I actually see you using your left hand. But if you aren't in 100 percent shape, you're due for a rough, tough evening."

So instead of running five miles as Ancil ordered, Max ran only until he came to a telephone.

He bribed his running mates to get lost while he chatted endlessly with Dorothy, telling her over and over that he would see her immediately after the fight, which he said would end before the sixth round. Irritated at being awakened so early, every morning, she chastised him for his lack of manners and advised him to spend more time with his book on etiquette. He did working much harder to master that subject than in getting ready for Schaaf. He slipped out of training camp at night to be with girls he had met since arriving in New York. Some of them had followed him to the campsite in upstate Orangeburg, staying in nearby motels. He didn't disappoint them, but he scared the hell out of Ancil when the morning paper carried a picture of him in a nightclub surrounded by an assortment of provocative beauties. He was supposed to have been sound asleep, resting for a new day of rigorous training.

"You're blowing it, Max," Ancil roared. "You work harder tricking me than doing what you're here for. If you are lucky enough to build up your strength in the daytime, you spend it all at night with women who don't care a damn about your future. Okay. Schaaf will teach you if I can't. "

On December 19, 1931 Schaaf did. Max lunged and spun and split the smoky air with a hundred screaming rights, sometimes turning himself into a corkscrew but leaving no leather on Ernie. He chased Ernie around the ring for ten rounds, and took a beating in the process. After five rounds he was too weak to fire another right and was forced to push Ernie away with his left. Of dire necessity he became a body puncher. But he was too weak at that game to do anything more with it than keep Ernie from running over him.

"I went the distance, and though I had to absorb a worse pounding than had been given to me in all my fights," Max wrote later, "I wasn't hurt. Just tired, never so tired before. Humbled? No, not me. I hadn't lost any faith in myself. I told Schaaf that I would pay him back the next time."

New York sportswriters loved Max. Who wouldn't, if your job was to have something lively and interesting to say in every edition, seven days a week? Max was the most colorful sports figure in town, along with Babe Ruth. Every time he opened his mouth a news story popped out. He wrote their stories for them. His antics in nightclubs, his chauffeured limousine rolling down Broadway with dancing girls leaning out of every window and Max waving from somewhere in their midst, his clowning in sparring matches all were liberally photographed and sprinkled on the pages of the numerous New York dailies. even the staid <u>New</u> <u>York Times.</u> But the reporters didn't let their enormous appreciation for Max get in the way of their judgement. To a man they thought he was a shooting star that would soon burn itself out.

Madison Square Garden officials thought Max had performed well enough with Schaaf to be given another chance, so Ancil signed him to fight Tom Heeney on January 16, 1931, less than a month later. This time Max, stung more by the ribbing he got from Dorothy than by the taunts the press for his failure with Schaaf, decided to get serious. He did his roadwork, stayed in camp and went to bed alone. It paid off. Heeney went through the ropes in the third round, having come into direct contact with the Baer right. It was a technical knockout. Max's growing throng of fans cheered long after he left the ring. Reporters said he looked a little better, but still "needed about 20 years of seasoning," as Max recalled.

Garden officials could count. They were particularly good at counting the gate, which was the same thing in those days without television as counting money. They had noticed that in two fights Max had drawn far bigger crowds than they were accustomed to seeing. So they wasted little time in persuading Ancil to agree to a February 6 fight against either Johnny Risko or Tommy Loughran. Risko, known as the "Rubber Man" because he seemed to be made of rubber when it came to absorbing punches, as well as because he was from Akron, was the world's leading pricker of fistic balloons. He would never be a champion himself, it was thought, but he was a champion trial horse for those who aspired to the top. I have already told you about Loughran. Ancil chose Loughran, as he told Max, because "you can learn something from being beaten by him, though either one can pin your ears back."

Max heard enough and read enough about Loughran to be impressed. The fight was set for only three weeks after the Heeney match, so he decided to be good and continue serious training after a three-day layoff, approved by Ancil, which he used to squire Dorothy to famous places by night and to romp with ladies of the musical stage by day. Dorothy chose this time to ask Max why he wanted to marry her when he had so many other girl friends. He answered that he was only teasing her, to see if she would notice and perhaps be jealous. She was not amused, which was good for Max. Her attitude made him more determined to beat Loughran.

It was not to be. The fight went the 10-round distance. Max said the only time he laid a hand on Tommy was when they touched gloves at the start of the first round. "He had 575 left hands in my face all night long and it was a long night," he told reporters. "Ancil warned me if I hit him six times in ten rounds I should get a Congressional Medal of Honor. He understated the case. He made me look and act so much like an amateur that I just had to stop and laugh, not my crazy laugh, but a laugh such as a fellow uses when he has tried his best, failed and isn't soured by his failure. It was my salute to a better man."

Max lost the fight but won yet more admiration from the fans and the press. Grantland Rice, dean of sportswriters, wrote these lines: "The boxing game has at least one heavyweight in sight. His name is Max Baer from Nebraska and California. He came east with a record of 110 knockdowns in 100 rounds and 24 KO's in 27 starts. However, when he was matched with Veteran Ernie Schaaf, a first class boxer who can also take his share of thumping, Baer lost the bout but more than made good with the crowd. He charged in on Schaaf like a wild buffalo and gave New York more actual fighting in a few minutes than it had seen all year."

Max did something after the Loughran fight that I've never heard of anyone else doing in the entire history of boxing. He dropped by his victorious opponent's dressing room and asked if he would give him a boxing lesson. "What's that?" Tommy asked, incredulously. "Show me how to use my left hand," Max said. "You hit me on the nose a thousand times tonight with your left. I'd like to hit someone else on his nose with my left. How about showing me?" When Tommy finally saw that Max was serious he agreed to meet him the next day for lunch and to work on his left in the afternoon. When the lesson ended Tommy told Max to "keep practicing, and you'll learn. All of a sudden you'll click. It will become a natural act, just as natural as swinging the right. You should learn to shorten your punches, too. A fighter with half an eye can see yours coming a mile away. Learn short punching and you'll be a hard man for anyone to beat from now on."

That meeting with Loughran produced another informational gem that would help Max get to the top. He asked Tommy who was the best short puncher around. "Jack Dempsey, without a doubt," Loughran said. Max immediately called on Dempsey, who he learned was staying at a certain hotel in town. Before making his unannounced visit to Dempsey's room he decided to deck himself out in his Gentleman's Attire #3 (afternoon dress), for he had read that Jack had been voted one of the world's ten best dressed men.

"Mr. Dempsey, I am Max Baer," my brother announced when Jack opened the door, tieless, vestless and shoeless. "Ambassador from where, sir?" asked Jack, inviting him in. Max laughed, knowing that Jack knew exactly who he was and what he was trying to do, make an impression. What he didn't know was that Jack also thought he wanted to make a touch, as so many others in the fight game did. When Jack asked how much he needed, Max fingered the $2 in his pocket and protested that money was the last thing he wanted from him. "Tommy Loughran told me you were the greatest short puncher the world has ever known. I want you to show me how you do it." Jack Dempsey needed no flattery, for he had soaked up as much of that as any fighter in history, but he was pleased, and agreed to do what he could then and there.

When Max stripped down, Dempsey looked at his shoulders and said, "plenty of power, but you'll never be much on short punching. You're a natural swinger. I'll show you short punching, but you won't learn much. When we get through with the short punching, I'll show you how to speed up your swings. If you can learn that trick, you can whip any man in the world."

During the half-hour lesson Jack warned Max, "I'm an old guy and all that, but listen, kid, if you try to slip anything over on me I'll use up the one punch I've been saving all these years and knock you right into the faucet end of the bathtub." Naturally, Max was sure he could and would do it, so kept his punching within reason. When it was over, Jack advised Max to change his swinging style. "You're swinging from your shoulders. Don't do that. Swing from the hip. Put your entire body into it. Pivot for every punch. Put your whole body into every punch." Max said later that this advice did more for him than anything he had ever learned about fighting. "It was the trick that made me a champion," he said.

The Garden wanted more of Max, but they failed to come up with names and terms that appealed to Ancil, who reasoned that his fighter was now the best drawing card in the business and it was his responsibility to make the most of it. Perhaps leaving New York would increase Max's value while he was away, and at the same time Max could capitalize elsewhere on the reputation he had developed in the Big City. He broke the news to Max with a sweetener. "It's time to go back home Max," he said. "I know that you would rather stay and take on the world and continue to make a fool of yourself with Dorothy, but believe me, you will make more money if we leave now. I suggest that we return to California by ship through the canal."

As he spoke, Max's face always a mirror image of his feelings first registered surprise, then disapproval, followed by a faint smile, a broadening smile, and finally a hearty laugh. "Ancil, you have more brains in your fingertips than I have where brains are supposed to be, so why should I object. Sure, I'll go. You make the arrangements and I'll be there."

It was the idea of an ocean voyage that appealed to Max. He had never been on a ship. More than that, it was the prospect of persuading

Dorothy to go along. He wouldn't let Ancil know until she was aboard, for he would surely cancel the whole project. Dorothy, to his delight, agreed, but limited the extent of her voyage to Havana, and in her own cabin at that, to his disappointment. On sailing day, after luggage had been taken aboard, Max informed Ancil that Dorothy would be a passenger, and that he needed $1,200 to get out of town without interference from the law. He owed that much to the hotel for extra room services, theater tickets and personal loans. He had promised to pay in full before going abroad. If he didn't, the law would arrive to escort him to court. For the first time in his career with Max, Ancil lost his cool and erupted with a torrent of purple prose and statements he didn't mean. Like abandoning Max to his fate and taking on a fighter with less talent but more brains. Half an hour later his fire cooled and he wrote out a check for Max to take back to the hotel.

The cruise to Havana was a romantic blockbuster for Max. He used his extensive wardrobe, still unpaid for, to impress not only Dorothy but 600 other passengers as well. Every two hours he appeared in a different costume, usually the wrong one, because shipboard dress was casual throughout the day until dinner. On the second day out Dorothy refused to sit with him at lunch until he changed into something more appropriate than formal morning clothes designed for an audience with the Queen of England.

Max did not forget that he was a boxer, possessed of a physique to turn every feminine eye.

He donned his training shorts and trotted fore and aft on the sun deck, stopping periodically to engage in shadow boxing. Pretty ladies politely clapped when he passed by. Men stared in envy. Dorothy boiled and fluffed her way off the ship at Havana with these parting words for Max: "Marry you? The world's greatest showoff! I don't need you."

Dorothy Dunbar, just before she married Max in 1934, joined him for a publicity trot in front of Ancil Hoffman's ranch near Sacramento.

ONWARD, UPWARD, OOPS

By the time the Baer entourage docked in San Francisco in early March 1931, Max had gone a full month without training, without dieting and without cares. Aboard ship he danced all night and ate all day, catnapping between meals. I too have experienced the glories of breakfast, lunch and dinner and between-meal snacks aboard the great ocean liners of the day, so I know it was impossible for Max to resist any of the sumptuous offerings. His nighttime frolicking, from ballroom to stateroom and back again, should have given him the exercise he needed to stay in shape. Evidently, it wasn't the right kind of exercise, because when he walked down the gangplank and into the streets of San Francisco, he was 25 pounds over his fighting weight.

"Max, you've lived the good life long enough and high enough to kill most mere mortals," Ancil told him. "Now you must get ready to fight again. I've signed you on to fight Ernie Owens on April 7 in Portland. We leave tomorrow, so tell your chicks goodnight tonight."

Max didn't complain, for some inner voice told him that he would need every day between then and the fight to shed 25 pounds and sharpen his punching. Portland was a pretty good fight town, but not as good as San Francisco or Oakland where he could be assured of a sell-out crowd. He thought it was terribly unjust that the California Boxing Commission ban on his fighting in the state was still being upheld. He would have to live with that unpleasant fact until August when the yearlong prohibition would end.

Owens lasted two rounds. In the first, he used Max as a punching bag, hitting him at will but to no avail. When the bell sounded Max turned to the crowd and pretended to comb his slightly rumpled hair and point with disdain at Owens in his corner. Laughter filled the hall. One minute later Max threw his first punch, a right uppercut to Owens jaw, and it was all over. The laughter turned to jeers, partly because the fans had seen little in the way of fighting, but probably more so because Max did not look good in winning. The fans felt shortchanged.

If the fight mob in Portland was displeased with Max, the crowd that watched his loss to Johnny Risko in Cleveland on May 5 was downright hostile. He chugged out of his corner in Round 1 like a heavy truck in first gear. Clearly he had a long way to go to regain his normal fighting weight of 203. Despite his ponderous movements, he clipped Risko hard enough on his left cheek to deck him for a nine-count. But from there on it was push, hold, shove, swing and miss and hold again. Neither fighter deserved a victory until Risko opened up in the ninth and 10th to tattoo Max's head and body with dozens of sharp but harmless blows, enough to give him the win. Some 8,000 voices articulated a sustained "boo" that was magnified several times by the low ceiling in the Cleveland Municipal Auditorium. On his way out of the ring Max made a show of plugging his ears with his fingers. The boos swelled in volume as he retreated to his dressing room, sounding, Max thought, like the snarls and yaps of an enormous wolf pack in hot pursuit.

That experience should have been harrowing enough to shake Max out of his lethargy. Cleveland's fight fans had delivered a clear message. They loved his antics, but only when he combined them with a good fighting effort. Max had no trouble understanding the message, but it came at the wrong time. Dorothy Dunbar had finally agreed to marry him on July 5 in Reno, the day after he was to fight the extremely tough Basque, Paulino Uzcudun. Dorothy would attend the fight, and he wanted to look good for her. That is, he wanted to come out of the fight without a scar to mar his handsome features. So he fought a defensive battle, and lost.

It was a 20-round affair, held in an outdoor arena on a blistering hot afternoon when the official temperature reached 110. Max weighed in at 203 and weighed out at 192. Jack Dempsey was the referee. Max thought that because he and Jack had become friends, and Jack had a very good opinion of Max's fighting abilities, even rounds would go to him. Not so. Jack was irritated with Max for not forcing the action. Paulino's style was to back away and counterpunch. If there was to be a fight, someone had to move forward. Max didn't, and for 20 rounds they clinched like wrestlers. Dempsey gave the fight to Paulino on grounds that he did a better job of fighting his normal fight than Max did with his. Max said afterward, "it was a lousy fight. We leaned on each other all afternoon. When Dorothy asked me why I looked so terrible in the ring, I told her I couldn't let that guy hurt my face. A guy can't get married with his nose plastered all over his face and a couple of black eyes." So he got married with his face, but not his reputation, intact.

Ten weeks later the California ban ended and Max won an eight round TKO over Jack Van Ney in Oakland. My friend Harry B. Smith, sports editor of the San Francisco Chronicle, had this to say about the proceedings:

"Max was a complete washout and you can write him off the books as a total loss. Baer, in the heyday of his fame, would have beaten a chap of the caliber of Van Ney in a round or so. Baer was lacking in practically everything that goes to make up a champion. He has no snap to his blows, was short with what he did swing, slow on his feet and tired at the close ... Max wasn't within 50 percent of the Baer who lost to Paulino Uzcudun last Fourth of July in Reno. He was so terrible that a lot of ringside folks thought he was carrying his opponent ... Just why Baer should fade away as he appears to have done is hard to explain. He's headed for the cellar, as they say of certain baseball teams."

From that, you would think Max lost the fight. In fact he battered Van Ney so badly in the eighth round that the referee had to call a halt. For most fighters, the victory would have been sweet. For Max, who knew how to read, it was as though he had won the battle but lost the war. Boxing critics expected far more from him in the way of style and dash, and he was not delivering what they felt he could deliver.

The truth is that Max didn't have his mind on his work. He and Dorothy were in a perpetual uproar. He had grown jealous of the many men she knew and continued to see. She was jealous of his popularity with other women. He walked out on her, she walked out on him. Seven times they separated and got back together. Max admitted that he had been unfaithful to her, but said it was only because he was sure she was stepping out on him. All of this was reported in the press and over the radio. They were called "The Battling Baers."

They were in the midst of their third separation when Max fought "Man Mountain" Jose Santa of Portugal, October 21 in Oakland. He did a lot to redeem himself. Santa outweighed him by 45 pounds and had a four-inch reach advantage, but Max wore him down with body punches, floored him in the ninth, and shattered him in the 10th with three knockdowns, the last of which left him unconscious. Max was scared that he had been badly hurt and rushed over to help care for him by rubbing his hands. Fortunately, he recovered quickly. Harry Smith wrote that Max looked better, but still lacked snap in his punching.

"Whatta I have to do to please these people?" Max complained to me. (By then I was 16 and as big as Max. Obviously, I was going to be bigger, and he had started treating me as his equal rather than as his little brother.) "Smith wants blood. They all want blood. It isn't enough that I knock out everybody I meet sooner or later. They seem to want a slaughter every time I step in the ring."

Max had a point. The same writers who deplored his ferocity the night Frankie Campbell was killed were now decrying his lack of ferocity. But I didn't let him know I agreed with him. Instead, I told him he had lost some of his natural grace in boxing and that he could easily get it back. He was, after all, that rare combination of slugger and speed merchant. Dancing and chipping away at his opponent was not his style, but by god he could move with the fastest men the ring has ever known, darting in like a striking snake, throwing his punch and recoiling to a safe distance with equal speed. It was this, I said, that the critics missed in his recent performances. From now on, I advised, he should concentrate on speed and footwork. The power in his right, and the remote threat of his left, would do the rest.

"Oho." roared Max. "My baby brother now thinks that because he weighs 205 that he can tell me how to fight. Tell me, little one, just how many people have you licked?"

"As many as you at my age," I responded. "None. But on the other hand I haven't run away from anybody either, and I don't intend to."

"Wow," Max shot back, "you pack one hell of a punch yourself with words. Listen. Buddy, you had my example before you, so you learned some things not to do, like not running away. But, you know, I think you have just now taught me something, too. Maybe its not so much what you do that impresses people, but how you do it. Okay, Buddy boy. I'm going to take your advice. From now on things will definitely be different. I'll give them victories with a flourish, victories with drama. You'll see."

His next fight was a rematch against Risko. It took place in San Francisco's new Seal's Stadium on November 18 - not the best time of year for an outdoor event. The rain came during the first of six scheduled preliminaries. By the end of the second match it was a downpour. More than 20,000 people were getting soaked, for the stadium had no protecting overhang. A chant from the crowd, "Bring on Max," grew steadily louder, until officials decided to do just that. They moved Max and Risko to the third slot in the program.

The fight went the 10-round distance and Max won in a walk, with several slides thrown in. The soggy under-footing didn't seem to bother Risko and his plodding strategy. But Max, executing swift strikes involving fast footwork, appeared to slip and catch himself on several occasions. He never fell, but he put on a good act of coming close. And it was an act, he told me later. "If they want drama, it's drama they will get." He dazzled Risko with speed and the best-left hand he had ever shown. Risko never caught up with Max, and never succeeded in hitting him with anything more than weak jabs. Max won nine rounds by lopsided margins. One round was even. Risko's face at the end looked as though he had fought off 20 fighters for 20 rounds. "If he keeps on improving at this rate," wrote Mr. Smith, "there will be something at the end of the rainbow for Max."

Ancil Hoffman had a great vocabulary and a fine wit, which he often combined with telling effectiveness in trying to get Max to change his errant ways. In the second Risko fight Max suddenly produced the kind of effort Ancil knew he could, and was non-plussed. "Maybe it was the rain," he said. "I've never known a fighter who liked to perform in a rainstorm, but maybe my Maxie is different in that way as in every other way. If so, we'll hold all of his fights outdoors in the middle of the rainy season and pray for a typhoon."

"It wasn't the dampness that brought out the best in me," Max said jokingly. "It was my kid brother. He's a better manager than you are, Pop. Maybe I should change."

"Maybe I should sign up Buddy and get rid of you," Ancil retorted. "He has your million dollar body, and then some, but he must have something on top of it called a head, unlike you, or how else could he persuade you to fight like the next world champion?"

I happened to be in the room during that conversation, and though I knew that Max and Ancil were kidding each other, I was nevertheless flattered, especially by Ancil's remark that I might be a fighter, too. Max had bought some gloves and I began to work out in an Oakland gym with my friends Hans Perkie and Jack Beasley. But I wasn't serious about it, for I had decided to attend Oakland Trade School and learn to be a plumber. Even so, I thought it was a good idea for the brother of the next world champion to know how to defend himself in the pugilistic arts.

Ten days after the Risko fight Max took on Les Kennedy in the Oakland Auditorium and put on display another weapon that led to a knockout in the third round. Remembering one of Jack Dempsey's admonitions when they were in New York, Max had quietly worked at putting his full body power into short punches. It was a series of these punches, with both hands, that caused Kennedy to drop his defense to protect his body. Max promptly nailed him with one of his patented haymakers. The count could have gone to 10 times 10 before Kennedy arose.

Max sent Dempsey a wire, telling him how beautifully he had carried out his instructions. He also invited Dempsey to attend his December 30 fight against Arthur de Kuh at the Oakland Auditorium. Dempsey accepted, and Max perversely horsed around for 10 rounds, using his left only on occasion and his new six-inch punch not at all. He won nine of the 10 rounds, but Dempsey was disappointed. "I must give Max bad luck," he said. "If I'm in the audience, or in the ring as referee, Max seems to think he must show off his acting skills and leave his boxing game in the gym."

Actually, Max didn't want to fight de Kuh, not because he was a threat, but because Max was arguing publicly with Ancil over his earnings for the year. He claimed he had earned at least $100,000 and hadn't received that much. Ancil said that counting debt repayment he had received more than his share. Max sued to get rid of Ancil and what was left of Ham Lorimer's contract. They settled the argument amicably, but not before the de Kuh fight. Max had his mind on other things that night, and fell back on what came most naturally to him - acting.

Max had a good year in 1932 - seven fights and seven victories, three by knockout. Maybe it was his best year ever, considering the quality of each opponent. Certainly it was the year in which he became a consistent two-handed fighter. His left was now a potent weapon, enabling him to keep his opponents off balance and set them up for his thunderous right. In fact, the power of his right and the memory of Frankie Campbell, haunted him in every match when he had rendered his opponent helpless and the referee was slow in stopping the fight. Fear of causing another death was deep in his gut. He never ridded himself of it, never wanted to rid himself of it, and in later years lost several fights he should have won because of it.

Outside of Max himself, the most colorful fighter in the heavyweight division in 1932 was Kingfish Levinsky, the "fish peddler" from Chicago. He possessed a looping right hand swing that sent many a fighter into the twilight zone. Among them was Tommy Loughran, who rarely hit the deck. Kingfish floored him three times in a

1931 match-up. Max took him on in Madison Square Garden on January 29, 1932. He made a nice bundle of cash, but that was the only good thing about the fight. Max took an easy decision, but every writer covering the event thought the 10-round affair was dull and uninteresting. I wonder. The King landed his famous overhand right square on Max's jaw twice without seeming to hurt him. Each time Max flashed his best smile at the audience and taunted Kingfish by sticking his jaw forward, inviting him to hit it again. It seems to me that would lift the fight out of the "dull" category.

Three weeks later Max was back in San Francisco, this time to fight Tom Heeney of New Zealand. More than 10,000 fans turned out at Seals Stadium for the afternoon imbroglio. Again, there was controversy. Max won seven of the 10 rounds. Two were even. Heeney was down for a nine-count in the fifth and the 10th. He took a solid battering in most of the other rounds, proving himself courageous and tough. Before the fight ended, the crowd began to make it known that they thought Max was carrying Heeney when he could easily put him away. Some of the writers thought so too. The Chronicle's Harry Smith disagreed, saying that Max "wouldn't know how" to carry an opponent. "He has too little experience for that." Max responded with what was becoming his standard defense of himself. "He was very brave. To knock him out I might have damaged him more than I wanted to. Some people would like to see that. Not me."

Max met Paul Swiderski of Syracuse, New York in the Los Angeles Auditorium on April 26. Paul's reputation as an effective slugger who could take it suffered badly that night. Max put him down for nine three times before the referee stopped it in the seventh. He totally dominated Swiderski, and he didn't play around in his normal manner, as the writers said in unison the next day.

Then came Mr. Walter Cobb on May 11 in the Oakland Auditorium. Cobb outweighed Max by 18 pounds and outreached him by three inches. He might as well have stayed home. Once again, Max was all business. In his enthusiasm for the fray he let a wild right get away, staggering Toby Irwin, the referee. Max ran to his side to see if he was hurt and to apologize, but Toby laughed and waved him back to battle. Cobb was completely outclassed. By the fourth round, after three knockdowns, he was having trouble seeing through the blood that ran freely from cuts above his eyes. Max looked pleadingly at Irwin, who then stepped in and stopped the slaughter.

Kingfish and his loud-mouthed sister, Lena, had been making sports page headlines ever since his fight with Max. Lena claimed that the King was not himself that night. The King said he would murder Max if they should meet again. Since he had won his subsequent fights impressively, support for a rematch gained ground. Max was willing, so Ancil signed him up for what was to be the last 20-rounder, to be held July 4 at an outdoor arena in Reno. It was a dilly.

The weatherman provided an afternoon temperature of 108 in the shade. God knows what it was in the sun, which blazed directly over the ring. I was sitting two rows back and figured it must have been at least 120. What a time to have to go 20 rounds!

Ernie Fliegel, a professional boxer in his youth, attended the fight and later described the hellish heat to <u>Oakland Tribune</u> sportswriter Alan Ward: "It was so hot, spectators developed blisters on their faces. Not sunburn blisters. Ice toted to the ringside for the fighters melted before it got there. The sun reflected off thousands of white-shirted-male spectators, causing a variation of snow blindness in the audience... The eye affliction, not damaging but distressing, was attested by physicians." He did not exaggerate. I thought the only way Max could survive (I was not concerned about the Kingfish) would be to make it brief with an early-round knockout.

Levinsky came out swinging, and missing. Max countered with a battery of hard rights and lefts to the body. Levinsky gasped audibly and clinched. Max backed away, catching the King with a left on the forehead as he moved out of range. A pattern was being established. Kingfish again advanced, aimed a right that whistled harmlessly past Max's nose. Max leaped in with both hands driving deep into Levinsky's midriff, and danced away. He let the Kingfish take the initiative, pacing himself for the grind ahead. Ancil had trained him well for this fight.

Lena was in very good voice. Her shouts of encouragement to her brother, and the epithets she launched at Max, could be heard above the thousands of other well-oiled vocal chords in the audience. If words were blows, Max would have gone down in the first round.

Despite Lena's entreaties, the Kingfish was taking a beating, round after round. He was dead tired by the 17th, and in the 19th landed on his back as Max connected with a terrific right uppercut to his jaw. He mustered enough strength to start the 20th with a flurry of swings. Max decided to stand toe to toe with him and slug-it-out tactic that could have spelled disaster for him if the Kingfish had been able to get some power into his punches. I think Levinsky did well to remain standing until the final bell. He was completely drained of energy, and had taken a pounding that few fighters could endure. The officials awarded the fight to Max by the lopsided score of 14 rounds to four with two even. The <u>Chronicle scored</u> it 17-2-1.

When Max's arm was raised in victory, Lena, who still was in great form, bellowed, "we've been fucked!" The Kingfish, standing in his corner, took a deep breath, looked at the burning sky and cried, "Whattaya mean, we've been fucked! I've been fucked!" The exchange was heard 40-some rows back. I know because the people in those rows let out a chorus of boos.

"The headiest fight he has ever made"..."Max was relentless"... "The finest bout Max Baer has ever fought." So said the reporters the next day. Kingfish also won praise. "They don't make any gamer fighter than he showed here this afternoon. How any heavy could withstand the merciless pounding administered by Baer is something that I cannot understand," said the <u>Chronicle's</u> Harry Smith. "Indeed, it may have a lasting effect on Levinsky and slow him down for future engagements, as Jeffries once killed off Tom Sharkey."

Max was not without words. "Ancil schooled me in pace for that mix-up," he said. "He showed me how to conserve energy. The results showed in the fight. I wasn't even drawing a long breath at the finish, but the Kingfish was wheezing like any fish out of water... It was just a nice workout for me."

Reporters had something else to review as a result of that fight. Hollywood had made the first sound movie of all the action. Associated Press liked the realism sound added to the camera work especially the "bawdy yelps" of Lena Levinsky and the closing remarks of both Lena and the Kingfish. I doubt that most of Lena survived the edited production that was shown in movie houses around the nation and the world. The language may be commonplace today, but in 1932 it definitely was not acceptable.

While in Reno, Max filed suit for divorce from Dorothy, claiming desertion. At the same time Dorothy filed in Los Angeles for divorce from Max, saying that he had used her as a sparring partner. She also demanded that he return $20,000 she said she had given him, in return for which she would not seek alimony.

This inevitable state of affairs came about, according to Max, when Dorothy found a note from one of his lady friends in his suit pocket.

Max described events leading up to the lawsuits in an article for the Oakland Tribune in 1934:

"I think she became what we will call 'professionally jealous.' When I met her I was the 'ham' fighter and she a former movie picture star. About six months after we married, Dorothy seemed to realize that she was an ex-actress married to a fighter who might get somewhere.

"I don't think she liked the idea. I was getting more of the spotlight than she was; people were seeking me out - not Dorothy - and you know how it is with girls who have been stars and aren't anymore.

"Dorothy began to get a little upset because the girls looked at me. She'd speak to me about it and I'd speak back; argument seven hundred and forty-seven would start; it would end, and then we'd kiss and make up and start all over again and be a couple of buddies for as long as four or five days.

"I can't recall the exact number of our actual separations and her threats to divorce me. What difference how many times? We were buddies again when I hit Hollywood to make the 'Prizefighter and the Lady' picture. But not for long.

"Could I help it if some nice, affectionate girls came along and said to me, 'how de do, Mr. Baer?' I couldn't. But Dorothy said I could. I said, 'say, you're just jealous, like I used to be. I got over it, and so will you.'

"That would start argument number 1,982 and after we were worn out vocally we'd kiss and make up and then get ready for number 1,983.

"All was going along okay - we weren't averaging any higher on the arguments than usual - when Dorothy found that note. Zowie! Evidence! So she announced she was going to sue for divorce and name a certain lady in an alienation suit - and out she lit.

"It seems that someone had been wanting her to do some acting for the screen at about that time, and a woman who writes about movies for newspapers took Dorothy in charge and told her suing me for divorce was okay, but naming the note-writing lady might injure Dorothy's future in the pictures. It was agreed accordingly that Dorothy would just sue me and not name anybody."

Less than a month after the suits were filed, Max and Dorothy made up again. "Everything's sweet," she told the press. For the next year or so it was alternately sweet and sour until sour prevailed. Divorce was granted in the autumn of 1933 - in Mexico. Two months later Max seriously considered challenging the validity of the divorce. Was a Mexican divorce legal in the U.S.? He was motivated by a desire to ward off a breach of promise suit by Miss Bee Starn, circus aerialist - "Girl on the Flying Trapeze" - for $150,000. Max swore he had never heard of her. Ancil believed him. Somehow, in ways I cannot remember, it all blew over and the divorce became final.

For Max, though, divorce did not mean "the end." He was surrounded by beautiful women who sought his full attention. Max gave it to them, one at a time. There was always at least one who interpreted his ardor as love that would lead to the alter, so he rarely knew a day when he was not beset by a breach of promise suit - real or threatened. He didn't worry about such things. Life was too pleasant for him to stop and fret about the excesses that made it pleasurable. But all the while, Dorothy was still in his mind. "I hankered for her," he told me.

Several weeks after the divorce he discovered that Dorothy was staying in an Oakland hotel. He went to a jewelry store and asked the owner, "how much to buy everything?" The answer, which required an hour or so for the owner to calculate, was $7,500. Max made a deal with him to pay $5,300 then and the balance that evening. Putting all the glittering stones and trinkets in his pocket, he headed for Dorothy's hotel.

She refused to see him in her room, saying that a divorce could become null and void "if we happen to be visiting, intimate like," but she did agree to go for a drive with him the next day. With Dorothy at his side, Max drove into an Oakland alley, stopped, and gave her the jewels. She threw her arms around Max and was telling him how wonderful he was when the car door opened and two process servers announced that they wanted the jewels. "You promised to pay the $2,300 owing on the stuff last night, and you didn't. So we trailed you."

Dorothy was chagrined and demanded an explanation. She was so heated about it that Max suddenly said he had had enough, got out of the car and walked away, not realizing that he was carrying Dorothy's lap dog. He put the dog on the ground and walked into town, leaving Dorothy to cope with the process servers and the car. But the dog, which knew him well, tagged along and wound up with Max at Ancil's Sacramento ranch for Thanksgiving dinner.

Just as the family was sitting down for the big feast a taxi rolled into the driveway and Dorothy popped out and into the house. Wagging a finger at Max, she said, "I want to see you alone." Max happily complied and they went to his room upstairs.

A short while later they returned. "Max says that you are to pay the $2,300 he still owes on jewelry he gave me," she said to Ancil. "It ain't Christmas yet," Ancil responded. "Even if it were, I wouldn't. Mr. Max Baer is so far overdrawn with me now that he'll have to live 200 years and fight every Tuesday to square me. I won't do any such thing, thank you."

Dorothy spun on Max and demanded, "you make him pay!" Max threw up his hands and was about to explain how powerless he was when Dorothy heard her pooch barking in an adjoining room. She tried to open the door. It was locked. Furious, she didn't bother to ask anyone to open it. She picked up a dining room chair and slammed it into the door, splintering both the chair and the door. "My goodness, how strong you are," Max exclaimed. "Maybe you should be my sparring partner after all." Dorothy whirled and left. She had taken the taxi all the way from Oakland, and now had to take it all the way back - an expensive outing, even by Dorothy's standards. I think that was the last time she and Max ever saw each other.

LIFE IN THE FAST LANE

After Max had so thoroughly whipped Kingfish Levinsky, promoters and sports writers around the country reassessed their evaluation of him and found that: (1) he was the most improved fighter among the heavies. And (2) he was the most popular in any division, and therefore the biggest attraction to fans willing to pay their way into an arena. Max knew where he stood and wanted to fight every week. Ancil knew better and said, "we'll fight only the best, for good money, in reverse order."

So Max had to wait nearly two months after Levinsky while Ancil arranged a return bout with Ernie Schaaf, who had given him a boxing lesson the first time around and was considered next in line for a championship shot. The bout was set for August 31, 1932 in the Chicago Auditorium. Betting odds favored Schaaf, two to one, despite the opinion of the press that Max had come farther than Ernie since their first encounter. Max explained after the fight how Ancil and Mike Cantwell helped him prepare:

"They said I should let him set the pace for five or six rounds, then steam up. I said I could flatten him in five if I stepped right out. 'You follow orders or I'll flatten you,' Ancil responded. I told him he could save his strength because I would follow orders."

He did follow orders, but he lost track of the rounds and almost saved his best until it was too late. "I had Schaaf a little groggy at the end of what I thought was the eighth round, but it really was the end of the ninth. I got confused, because I was looking at the clock while in my corner after the round, and it said 'nine.' I thought that meant the round coming up, whereas, in Chicago, they don't show the round to be fought until the bell rings for it.

"When I answered the bell I figured it was the ninth and not the tenth, and I kept punching Schaaf around and softening him up for a final round rally. I noticed there was some excitement in my corner, and it wasn't until about a minute before the round was over that I got the message that I was fighting the last round. Then I broke loose with everything I had and succeeded in flattening Schaaf.

"He was out for about 10 minutes, but I didn't get credit for a knockout- only won on decision- because the knockout came about five seconds before the bell."

Max didn't know it then, but in time he would be credited for something he repeatedly denied was true- the blow that supposedly led to Schaaf's death six months later in a fight with Primo Carnera. Primo knocked out Schaaf in the 13th round with a punch that writers said had no sting at all to it. They noted that Primo had not really hit Schaaf hard all night. How to explain that Ernie never woke up following his K.O.? Easy. Blame it on Max's 10th round knockout punch six months earlier.

Nathaniel S. Fleischer, then editor of Ring magazine, saw fit to repeat this speculation in a piece he did on Max in 1940. "To this day" he said, "it is maintained by experts that Schaaf never fully recovered from that devastating wallop, and that Ernie's death later on was due to the injury he sustained in Chicago."

Even today, Ring record books include the phrase, "badly injured in his fight with Max Baer," in their account of Schaaf's career. How do they know? They don't! And it's unfair to guess on such a matter. I remember that Max was worried at the time of the knockout, because several minutes (the exact number has been reported variously) elapsed before Ernie came out of it. He was relieved when Ernie said he felt fine. Was Ernie talking nonsense? I don't think so, because he fought four times before he met Carnera, and won them all.

It is grossly unfair to try and pin a second death on Max for a punch that landed six months before Ernie's death - six months that included 53 rounds of tough fighting by Ernie before he caught the actual punch that killed him.

I know from personal experience that you can knock a man out and wonder how it happened. The victim was Red Fields, who I fought in Des

Moines in 1934. The first round was only about one minute gone when I unloaded a roundhouse right in the direction of Red's head - and missed, I thought. But to my astonishment he went down, out cold. I accused Ancil of fixing the fight, because I was sure I hadn't hit Fields. He told me I was crazy, but I didn't get the idea out of my head until I saw a picture in Ring magazine several weeks later that showed my glove snapping Field's head back on his shoulders. I had clipped him on the chin without feeling it. So I say to myself that Carnera may have hit Schaaf with an apparently innocuous punch that in fact was harder than it looked to the press.

If indeed Schaaf died from injuries sustained before he fought Carnera, I would like to suggest that Max was only one of many who fought him. To say that Max alone was responsible is to play God. Who knows what the accumulated affect of all Ernie's fights might have contributed to that fatal moment in the 13th round of his February 10, 1933 fight with Primo Carnera in New York City?

Max closed out the year 1932 with a perfect record of seven wins in seven bouts - three by knockout. The last took place in Sioux City, Iowa on September 26 against Tuffy Griffith. On that same night, some 1,500 miles to the east, in New York City, his next opponent, the one who would propel him into a championship fight, Max Schmeling was defeating one of the toughest fighters of the time, Mickey Walker. Max was fully aware of what was going on in Madison Square Garden, for he had his eyes on "der udder

Max." To show his readiness for the German hero, he made mincemeat of Mr. Griffith, slapping him all over the ring for six rounds, including a knockdown, and rendering him helpless in the seventh. The referee - not without some prodding by Max - stopped it and declared Max the winner by a knockout. He didn't fight again until the following June 8 - a night that will live forever in the Baer household.

Personally, Max Schmeling was a nice guy. I met him many times and talked of many things. I never heard him cast aspersions on anybody because of race, which doesn't mean that he hadn't done so in comments to others as the press had reported. Whether he was a racist or not, he carried the aura of his Fatherland and the racial superiority dogma of the ruling Nazi party. It was said, perhaps to build up the gate, that he considered any American, regardless of color, as ethnically inferior to the pure Arian strain he supposedly represented.

Max made the most of the situation by adorning his boxing trunks with the Star of David and telling the world how proud he was of his Jewish blood. But it wasn't all show. Max believed he was going into battle with an arrogant symbol of the "master race." Max Schmeling was the first and only fighter Max Baer ever hated before meeting him.

The fight was staged in Yankee Stadium before a crowd that paid some $300,000 to watch the "Battle of the Decade." Promoter Jack Dempsey astutely, but quietly, encouraged the advance publicity that pitted an American Jew against a German Nazi Jew-hater.

My brother was the sentimental favorite, but hard-nosed bettors and New York writers were not impressed with his preparations for the fight. Max hardly ever looked good in training. The expert knew that, but when they compared his readiness with that of Schmeling, they found Brother Max wanting. Most of them wrote that the German's durability, sharp shooting ability and excellent right hand power would be too much for him to handle. So much for the experts.

In round one my brother rushed at Schmeling with ferocity he had never before displayed. He quickly smashed a fierce looping right to his head. Schmeling was staggered and held on by clinching until the referee broke it up. Schmeling then kept Max at bay for the rest of the round with his beautifully educated left hand. In all the rounds that followed Max was the aggressor, but in his burning desire to end it early he swung wildly and hit Schmeling low in the second, fourth, fifth and seventh rounds. All of those rounds were awarded to Schmeling. At the start of the eighth Ancil told Max to let go with everything he had. Schmeling, who had fought gamely and had made few mistakes of his own, was suddenly overwhelmed by a flurry of lefts and rights thrown by Max without regard for Schmeling's famed counter-punching. He stopped for an instant, measured Schmeling before he could recover, and shot a paralyzing right to his head. Schmeling seemed to collapse into a clinch, barely able to stand, and the bell rang.

Schmeling's courage was on display for all to see in the ninth. Somehow he reached into his inner resources and drew out enough strength to ward off Max's rushes and retaliate with his brilliant left hand - a hand that seemed to have a life of its own and which won the round for him by a narrow margin.

Two sports writers described the 10th round. Nat Fliescher reported it this way: "Baer went after his opponent like a wildcat. In vain Schmeling tried to hold him off with jabs. Baer wouldn't be denied, rushed, swung, hooked, and threw punches galore into the German's face and body. Some of Baer's wallops missed, but the majority of them got home. Schmeling, groggy and exhausted, was beaten to the floor. He arose at the count of nine and Baer charged in again, battering him to a neutral corner. Schmeling was helpless; his arm dangling by his side as Baer spun him half-round with a sizzling right to the jaw. (Then) Max held back - thinking of Frankie Campbell as he muttered an appeal to the referee to stop the slaughter." Referee Arthur Donovan did.

Westbrook Pegler, a fine sports writer before he went into politics, described the main blow this way: "A sucker's wallop suddenly arched through the atmosphere made milky by tobacco smoke and resin dust, and took Schmeling on the jaw with a squashy sound and a spray of moisture. Schmeling's neck seemed to snap. His body went-limp, his legs spread and his arms fell as he swayed against the ropes. Baer's seconds, Ancil Hoffman and Mike Cantwell, howled insanely at him to go on punching." Max did, of course. Schmeling had "lost his bearings, ran into a lot more swings to the head, went down, got up, and was presently led to his corner by a referee who had good reason to fear that another blow might take his life."

Max trains at his New Jersey camp in preparation for his fight with Schmeling. His sparring partner is unidentified, but Jack Dempsey, his adviser (far side of ring) and his trainer, Mike Cantrell, look on.

After the fight, Schmeling blamed the heat for his loss. He had been narrowly ahead on points until the 10th, but four of the rounds in-his- favor had been given him because of Max's low blows. All were rounds that Max otherwise would have won.

Max said that his fight to get from the ring to his dressing room was harder than the fight itself. He glowed with pride and assurance. "Boys," he told the press, "I'm going to win the championship!"

The Baer clan at the home of Jake and Dora Baer (seated), listening to the radio broadcast of Max's fight with Max Schmeling. They seamed pleased, as well they should have been.

The town of Livermore went wild. Newspaper and radio people swept into the place to interview Mother and Dad. Associated Press quoted Mother this way: "My Mickie! I knew he would do it. I knew. There have been some aspersions cast on my boy's Jewishness. You just tell those people in New York that Maxie has got a Jewish father, and if that doesn't make him Jewish enough for them, what will? That'll show them".

THE BEST OF TIMES

For up to half of America's unemployed and under-employed work force in the middle of 1933, it certainly was not the best of times. The great depression was in its fourth year, but Franklin D. Roosevelt had been inaugurated president in March and had told us that we had "nothing to fear but fear itself." The National Industrial Recovery Act had been launched; millions marched in cities across the nation, carrying the "blue eagle" symbol of industrial strength and national hope. Dozens of other alphabetical agencies were being created daily to help various segments of the population - farmers, consumer cooperatives, small businesses, students, even artists and playwrights and actors.

The mood of the country was upbeat, and that was precisely the situation in which Brother Max found himself after his dramatic defeat of Max Schmeling in June. Now he was the Number 1 contender for the heavyweight title held by Primo Carnera, the biggest man at six feet, six inches and 267 pounds ever to have sat on that auspicious throne. That fact alone, however, would not have accounted for the extraordinary place Max occupied in the national consciousness. Many great fighters had preceded him without causing a stir outside the world of fans of the sport. Max was now literally a star of stage and screen, and admired by a cross section of the nation for his wit, style, personality and manly abilities.

A popular limerick of the time, author unknown to me or the papers that printed it, summed up his status:- There was a young scrapper named Baer who had the most beautiful hair, He could flirt, he could fight, He could dance all the night, That fantastic fast puncher, Max Baer. That frivolous fighter named Baer Had the ladies all up in the air, He would love 'em and leave 'em, And blithely deceive them, That bewitching young biffer, Max Baer.-

Max Fleischer, editor of Ring magazine, wrote that my brother was "a brilliant conversationalist; he shines as a true master of repartee. I've seen him time and again, walk into a room crowded with the best wits in town, engage in a rapid-fire series of wise cracks and leave them all limp and speechless for want of words to combat his airy persiflage."

At a press conference in New York he was asked who he thought the next heavyweight champion would be. "Every time I look in my crystal ball I see my own reflection, he answered. "Do I believe in crystal balls? Maybe not, but I do believe in balls, and I've got em -enough to beat anybody in the world."

He always referred to reporters as "boys-." "Boys," he said on another occasion when he thought he had been badly misquoted, "you've given me a lot of trouble at times, and I deserve it. Now I'm going to give you some trouble, and you deserve it. From now one my name is Max 'No Comment' Baer."

Cocktail chatter at a party one night hit on the idea of one world. "Boxers see a lot of people from all over the world," said a chorus line beauty from Havana, speaking to Max. "Do you think we'll ever have a real League of Nations?" "I'm happy to just be in the same world with you," Max replied. "I'd be even happier if the world were bounded on the east by your place and on the west by my place. That's my idea of one world." She agreed that would be cozy, but added, "If you were as good at evading punches as you are at ducking questions, you would be the champion." Max glowed with satisfaction.

So fetching was Max as a stage personality that Billy Rose, one of Broadway's most successful impresarios, gave him a featured spot in a 1933 musical revue and paid him the handsome sum of $3,500 a week to dance, joke and make jolly with some of the world's most beautiful showgirls. Before making that plunge, however, he had already established himself as a movie performer of surprising ability. The picture was titled "The Prizefighter and the Lady."

Max agreed to do the film not only because of the money and the opportunity to display his out-of-the-ring acting ability before millions, but also because it was the only way he could get to know Primo Carnera - and perhaps persuade him to put his title on the line. Ancil had been trying for weeks to talk Primo's numerous managers into *signing for* a title fight with Max, to no avail. Primo was enjoying the good things of life that come with the championship, and so were his managers. Max was too big a gamble, and as long as the boxing commission didn't push him into meeting Max, he would just as soon not.

Then Hollywood called. They had a great idea for a movie featuring a reigning heavyweight champion, and his Number-1 challenger. Why not use the real-life protagonists (except for the lady) to play the lead roles? Primo said yes, but only if the main fight scene (the script called for him to lose) allowed him to look good in losing. Max, of course, needed no persuasion. Not only would his lady be Myrna Loy, one of Hollywood's leading actresses and a beautiful one to boot, but the rest of the cast would include such luminaries as Walter Huston playing his manager, Otto Kruger as gangster Willie Ryan, Jack Dempsey as the fight referee, and Lupe Valez as an all-round siren. The picture would be produced by Hunt Stromberg and directed by W. S. Van Dyke -both at the top of the Hollywood heap. What a glorious opportunity!

The plot was simple and depended on the characters to make it work. Myrna Loy was the mistress of Kruger's gangster, Willie Ryan. Max was a rough pug with a big punch who was aiming for a shot at Primo, the champion. Huston was a perpetually frustrated manager who couldn't keep his fighter out of the night club circuit or get him to take fighting seriously. Loy fell for Max, who stole her from Kruger. Kruger, instead of ordering Max snuffed out; commanded him to be a good husband- he loved Loy too. But Max, beset by many women, found himself unable to let most of them alone. Loy went back to Kruger. His disillusioned manager also walked out. So when Max entered the ring to meet Primo, he was on his own. He was losing the fight 'when, lo, his wife and manager returned. Max rallied to win the championship and live happily ever after with Loy.

The basic story, straight out of real life, worked marvelously well as fiction. It was to be expected that the professional actors would do a polished job and that the direction would be fast-paced and crisp. Max was the surprise."Confident natural"..."able to express emotion"..."A pleasant shock to Hollywood" were some of the reviewers' comments in describing Max's performance.

Max was delighted with everything that happened to him in Hollywood. He was adored by stars and starlets, and lived up to his reputation by entertaining a countless number of them in his dressing room, or the girls, during working hours and, of course, after. In the so-called "life story" he wrote for the Oakland Tribune he confessed that he "got a great kick out of acting. I may stick to acting altogether. It's what you can call steady employment, no road work, and you are always sure of having some nice affectionate pals."

The picture was premiered simultaneously in New York and San Francisco on November 19, 1933. Max appeared on stage before every showing the first three days in San Francisco. He did his best with gags, mugging, shadow boxing and just plain showing off to prove that he was in fact everything the film depicted him to be, the audience ate it up. As predicted by the critics, "The Prize Fighter and the Lady" became one of the big moneymakers of the year.

He went directly into the Billy Rose production, and after about three months of cavorting on the New York stage remembered his main occupation. It had been nearly eight months since the Schmeling fight - time to get on with the pursuit of the title. Ancil went to work again with Primo's managers, and this time came away with a contract to stage a title defense on June 14, 1934 at the Madison Square Garden Bowl in Long Island City. He would have three months to get ready.

Two underworld types are handled easily by Max in the movie, "The Prizefighter and the Lady." Max's natural acting ability helped make this film one of the top romantic comedies of the year.

Max claimed that even though his movie fight with Primo was carefully worked out to a prearranged conclusion and that both he and Primo had agreed not to pull any surprises on each other, he nevertheless learned a lot about Primo's style. "We didn't make that (fight) scene all in one day," he said in his. "Life Story." "Every day when we were to do another round or so, Primo's manager would come to Ancil and myself and say. 'No monkey business! No hard punches! If you punch hard, I will never agree to give you a fight.' So what could I do? ... But I didn't waste the time I was clowning with him. I kept watching for his weaknesses. One of them, I found, was that when I'd shoot a left to his head his guard would go up - high! I was pleased to know that."

Max's first movie, "The Prizefighter and the Lady," 1934, at his best. In this scene he is shown with co-star Myrna Loy as he prepares to do battle with the real-life champion, Primo Carnera, in a remarkable fictional forecast of the actual fight the two men would have later that year. Walter Huston, his manager in the movie, is at the lower left.

Max did something else to improve his chances. He decided to get serious about training. "When I went to Asbury Park (New Jersey -the training site) my chief ambition was to get in plenty of roadwork," he said in his story. "That's what I had ducked doing all through the other years. It's a terrible grind. Up early in the morning, walk a mile, gallop a while, sprint, walk, gallop, sprint. It's monotonous, and in other fights I never felt I needed it. Always had plenty of confidence in my punch.

"But the Carnera fight was different. To win meant dreams that would come true - champion of all the fighting champions of the world. Every thought of it made me more and more serious and Ancil Hoffman, my manager, couldn't figure out whether I was screwier than ever, or just playing some new kind of joke when I began yelling that what I wanted most of all was road work.

"Ancil just couldn't do anything but remember the days and the years when I started out on the road, bribed or shook off my companions, and just went prowling around for a good looking lady face instead of jogging and improving my speed, my wind and building up my muscles. But at Asbury I wore smoke glasses and blinkers."

It's crazy. Max was doing the best job of his career in preparing for a fight. But Bill Brown, chief honcho and big mouth of the New York Boxing Commission, chose to think otherwise. He kept issuing public warnings to Max that unless he shaped up the commission would postpone or cancel the fight. I think that Bill Brown was not looking at Max the challenger, but at Max the nightclub comedian and Hollywood heavy. Max put it this way in his story:

Brown visited my camp a week before I met Carnera and got his name and picture in many papers by saying that I was in horrible condition, that I was a bum, and that unless my mix-up with Carnera was called off the public would be bunked, paying big money to see the big Italian bat me out in a round or so.

"The afternoon Brown arrived, I was tipped off that he was a very fussy old fellow and that he had practically ordered that I do my best. If I had done my best I would have knocked out every sparring partner I had - maybe sent the whole gang to the hospital. So, I said, 'who the hell is this guy Brown to tell me how to do my training? I will do as I please, and that will have to satisfy the whole Brown family.'

"I did as I pleased and Brown nearly had apoplexy. I am called a 'butcher' but no one every heard of me slaughtering sparring partners. They are my buddies, and I am not out to get a reputation by wrecking them. They are either young fellows, like myself, who have ambition, but unlike myself, haven't had the opportunity, or old-timers trying to earn a few dollars with what skill they have left.

"I put on my regular show for Brown. He didn't like my clowning. He must have chewed his palate when I let the boys get some cheers for themselves by allowing them to poke me around the ring. I'm supposed to be a spotlight hound. Okay, but I won't grab it by hurting my sparring partners.

"I'll always feel that Brown let loose the blast about my being unfit not so much because he thought I was really out of shape physically, but because I ruffled his tail feathers with a workout according to my ideas - not his."

Max wrote those words after he had won the championship and before he lost it. He didn't mention that Brown carried his tirade against him from the training camp to New York City, where one day before the fight he tried to get the commission to cancel it. He was outvoted two to one, but he proved to have a long memory. In 1937 he was instrumental in getting Max suspended in the State of New York, forcing Max to do what he probably would have done in any event - go to England to carry on his career.

Bill Brown didn't realize it, but his pre-fight complaining about Max's condition did Max a great favor. One of Max's psychological strategies was to lull Primo into thinking that he was out drinking a quart of booze every night and sleeping all day. What he really did was to show up at a nightery, drink ginger ale from shot glasses, and get his picture in the paper with one or more lasses sitting in his lap. I was in camp with Max and I know that his trickery worked. Word from Carnera's camp was that Primo was highly pleased with developments. Primo didn't know that one of Max's training routines was to lift me in the air repeatedly to strengthen his arms, and I was just about as big as Primo.

I think that Max would have won the fight easily if none of this had happened. If any strategy worked to his practical advantage it probably was a piece of advice passed on to Ancil by one of his sports writer friends shortly before the big event. The sports writer had observed that boxing was the only sport in which the participants did not warm up before going into action. He noted that most knockouts occurred in the first or second rounds, before the fighters were limber; that baseball pitchers warmed up before starting; that tennis players did the same; that football players who had been in the game for some time received fewer injuries than fresh replacements. Ancil was quick to get the message, and with Jack Dempsey's concurrence planned to have Max work up a sweat by shadow boxing in his dressing room just before going into the ring.

The plan was carried out to the letter. Fight time arrived. Max did his thing. He was warm all over when he donned his dressing gown and walked to the ring. To his amazement, Carnera, the champion (champions normally enter last) was already there. Not only there, but he had been there five minutes, sitting on his stool in the cool air of a damp evening. Max said later, "It is not good for a big man to be sitting out in the starlight with the danger of getting hit by drops of dew."

Betting odds were seven to five in favor of Carnera. Sportswriters covering his camp called him "vastly improved"... "owner of a dynamite left, so good he doesn't need the right." Boxing legend Tommy Burns pronounced him in "top shape." He weighed 260 pounds - 52 more than Max -and had a four-inch height advantage (6' 6-1/2" to Max's 6' 2-1/2"). He had an 80-inch reach compared to Max's 81" and was one year older at age 26.

Ancil's instructions to Max-as they awaited the opening bell went like this, according to Max: "Now you are nice and warm. We all hope that dear Primo is the same. But maybe he isn't. The way for you to find out if he is brittle is to gallop in the first chance you get and singe his beard. Be liberal with him. Give him a good $2.50 singeing. Then step back fast or you may be crushed with a falling mountain range."

The bell rang. Primo lumbered to the center of the ring, then Max rushed him straight from his corner, flicked a few lefts, jockeyed him around for about 10 seconds, then unloaded a flashing right that traveled the full possible distance en route to Primo's chin. He tottered and crashed to the canvas like a fallen-tree. At the count of nine he pulled himself up and got his gloves in line with his face when Max drove a straight right through his defense directly to the front of his jaw. Another crash as Primo hit the floor. The big guy managed to rise again and stay away from Max until the bell rang.

Aside from Primo's nosedive, the most arresting feature of the first round was the behavior of referee Arthur Donovan. Ancil had voted against using him, on grounds that he was hostile to Max and showed it in the Schmeling fight. He was outvoted, and true to form, there was Arthur getting in Max's way each time Carnera rose to his feet, preventing a possible first round K.O.

Max reflected in his story that "I will always feel that I could have put him away in the opening round if Arthur Donovan had not been jumping around the ring so that he interfered with my free movement and halted me from keeping right on top of Carnera before Primo ever had a chance to recover from my pile driver rights."

Courageous Primo came back in the second to land several lefts on Max's head, but Max won the round with a punishing body attack. In the third Max continued his barrage to Primo's midriff and chest, taking a few head shots in exchange, and decked his man with a wicked left as the round ended. Max rested in the fourth and lost it because of Primo's numerous harmless but point-making lefts to his head. Primo began the fifth with his best punch of the night, another left to Max's head, but this one stung. Max retaliated with more body punches and a crashing right to his mouth that drew spurts of blood. Primo went into a series of clinches until the bell.

There were no knockdowns in the sixth, but it was the nearest thing to a real contest in the entire fight. Primo came out slugging and forced Max to the ropes. Max slipped away and pelted him with a rapid series of lefts and rights to his body and head. Donovan again got in the way. Max grazed Donovan's shirt trying to reach Primo's jaw with his right. It was his round.

Max took it easy throughout the seventh, and lost it. He didn't force much action in the eighth, but won it by a slight margin. In the ninth he began to pick up steam, but noticed that his newspaper friend Harry B. Smith of the <u>San Francisco Chronicle</u> had slumped over his typewriter. He leaned over the ropes and yelled for someone to take care of him, then went back to the task of pulverizing Primo. Max was not showboating. He cared a lot about Harry, and thought he was having a heart attack. It was Max at his best.

In an earlier round Max actually did a bit of outrageous showboating. When the bell sounded for the start, he slipped while leaving his corner and decided he didn't have enough resin on his shoes. He ambled casually over to Primo.'s corner, turned his back on Primo, flashed a smile at Primo over his shoulder, and proceeded to rub his shoes in Primols resin. Then he sauntered back to mid-ring and thanked the astounded Primo before belting him in the chops. Of such stories are legends made. I saw this one. It was widely and humorously reported.

The ninth round went to Carnera because of a questionable low blow, called by Donovan. But Donovan excelled himself in the 10th. Max had returned to outright, fierce aggression, slamming rights and lefts at will into a nearly defenseless Carnera. The man mountain fell to the canvas three times. When he rose the last time Donovan stepped between them stared into Primo's eyes for 10 seconds or more, and then waved them back to battle. But the bell rang before another punch was thrown.

Primo Carnera, as incredibly courageous as any fighter in history, crashed to the deck five more times in the 11th as Max smashed him all over the ring. He rose for the 11th time and moved blindly toward his tormentor before Donovan called the fight and proclaimed Max the new heavy weight champion of the world.

When all the hoopla in the ring calmed down enough for him to escape (but not before telling the radio world how much he loved Mother and Dad and Bernice and Frances and Livermore), Max made his way, partially on the backs and hands of a phalanx of fans, to a dressing room already crowded with newsmen and radio announcers. "Well boys," he greeted them, "don't you think I deserve a beer before we get down to your questions?"

Press accounts of the fight were unanimous. Max was the most exciting heavyweight since Dempsey in his prime. He was said to have more speed than any fighter since Corbett. The quality of his repartee and wit had no parallel in the history of boxing. And, most important, his right hand was even more destructive than Dempsey's - the most lethal ever.

Speaking of Max's power Paul Gallico, the eminent sportswriter, wrote that the inept Donovan had, through his mistakes, saved Carnera from probable death. He put it this way:

"I am convinced that an official blunder may have prevented a killing. When referee Arthur Donovan stepped between Baer and Carnera in the 10th round and for 15 seconds gazed into Primols unseeing eyes, in the meantime holding Baer off, he unwittingly may have prevented a repetition of the terrible death of Frankie Campbell. Because Carnera was then propped up against the ropes, out on his feet, hands down, chin out, exactly as Campbell was in his fight with Baer ... I call it an official blunder because Donovan had no right to permit the fight to go on once he stepped between the men. As long as Carnera was on his feet, Baer had the right to hit him. As soon as the referee stepped between them, the fight was technically over, with Baer the winner. Donovan waited so long he gave the shocked Primo a chance to recover and robbed Baer of a clean-cut K.O. in the 10th. But he also saved the Italian's life by doing so."

I suppose that in our youth most of us have imagined how we would go out into the great wide world, become famous and successful then return to our hometown to bask in the adulation of our family, friends and teachers who never imagined that we had such talent. It happened to Max, and I was one of the beneficiaries, when the Baer family returned to Oakland after the Carnera event. Dad and I were in New York for the fight. Mother came east to be a part of the victory celebration at a plush Manhattan hotel. Some 40 people attended the gala dinner. Many big names in boxing, show business and the press were there. Ancil picked up the tab. A few days later we boarded the train for the long trip home (three days and three nights via the Broadway Limited and the City of San Francisco).

Four "welcome home" celebrations were held successively by the cities of Livermore, San

Leandro, Oakland and San Francisco. Parades confetti, banquets, speeches, cameras, radio and newspaper interviews, and lots and lots of thank-yous. Max was superb, exhibiting for the first time in years his youthful bashful streak, then glowing with confidence about the future, rattling off enough witticisms to fill the sports pages for days to come. He told one crowd that he would keep the title until I was ready to inherit it (a surprise to me, for I had not yet decided to become a boxer). So I too basked in glory -of the reflected kind.

By this time I had finished my work at trade school and was contemplating a career as a plumber. My exposure to boxing as a visitor to Max's training camps and several of his fights hadn't given me any ideas about trying to make a living that way. In any case, Mother would have been against it. Plumbing was safe and sane, and plumbers were among the aristocrats of labor. So I was getting started doing small jobs as a helper, when a change in the housing code also changed my life.

I paid no *attention when* the code suddenly required houses to be built not more than 16 inches off the ground. That was the business of designers and carpenters, not plumbers. Then I got a job helping a master plumber install pipes in Ancil's new mini-mansion in Sacramento. We had to do some of the work under the house. The plumber crawled under and called for me to follow with the tools. I lay on my back and inched my way until I became stuck and unable to move forward or backward. The floorboards had to be torn up to get me out. Very embarrassing, but the experience taught me that I was too big to be a plumber.

While I was pondering my dilemma, Max and Ancil came up with a very attractive proposal. Max was about to start an exhibition tour of the North and Midwest. Why not come along and be his sparring partner? It would be a lot of fun for me, Max would save money by not having to pay $25 a day for sparring practice, and who knows, maybe the spectacle of the Brothers Baer in the same ring might prove to be good box office? of course, I readily agreed.

I wasn't a total novice in fisticuffs. Some time earlier I had let a little of Max rub off on me and decided that I, as his brother, ought to know at least enough about fighting to defend myself. Max wasted no time. He took me to a sporting goods store in Oakland and bought me the works - gloves, shoes, shorts, sweat suit and punching bag. I took all of this equipment to a gym and started working out on my own. Two friends, Hans Perkie and Jack Beasley - both former fighters - stopped by occasionally to give me a few tips. Every now and then Jack would get in the ring with me and demonstrate footwork, jabs and other elementary things. But to me it was all just fun. I was not serious.

Thanks to Hans and Jack (Max never taught me a thing about boxing up to that time) I was reasonably well equipped to become a sparring partner. My size was surely no handicap. I was now taller than Max and outweighed him by 20 pounds. By reason of physique alone I would have been an imposing opponent.

The tour went up to Vancouver, B.C., on to several smaller cities in that magnificent Canadian province, down to Spokane, over to Seattle, south to Portland and back to California by way of Eureka. Ancil's feeling about the potential box office value of Max and me sparring together was fully vindicated. Throngs of fight fans turned out to watch us mix it up. Before long it became evident that our sparring was attracting more attendance than Max's exhibitions with local heroes.

I have some personal reservations about the exhalted status of Ancil Hoffman as a boxing manager, but I certainly do not fault his canniness. Within a week of the start of our tour in Vancouver he put me on the schedule as Max's exhibition opponent in a series of two-rounders. As he expected, we played in standing room only. One of the reasons for our success, aside from the fact that Max was the champion and I was his brother, was the unexpected roughness of our bouts. Max was a slugger. I tried to box. He had always been willing to take any number of punches to land one of his own. I operated on the principle that it was better to hit than be hit. In so doing I antagonized Max to the point that he would really throw dynamite punches and I would retaliate. Ancil saw fit to call off the Brothers Baer act.

In its place there would be two Baer acts - one by Max and his opponent, one by me and mine. It started in Eureka. Ancil informed me when we arrived in town that instead of fighting Max in an exhibition I would fight a guy by the name of Tiny Abbott in an official, registered bout, scheduled for 10 rounds. I remember my response: "You mean I am going to lose my virginity? "You sure are," said he. "Tiny beat Max on a foul the first time they fought, and shoved him around for six rounds the second time before Max knocked him out. He's no pushover."

I was anxious that my first recorded fight be a victory. Tiny started the action with a swing at my head that missed. I countered with a blistering right to his stomach that lifted him off the canvas. He sank to a sitting position, gasping for air, until he was counted out.

"Hey Max, how come you had so much trouble with that guy?" I taunted my brother afterward. "Couldn't you handle him? Was he too fast for you?" Max sputtered and mumbled something about Abbott being four years older and all washed up. So it was that my first fight was with a common opponent, but it would not be the last - nor would it be the last time I would dispatch such an opponent quicker than Max did, nor the last time I would rub it in, nor the last time Max would react in much the same way. A rivalry - perhaps the friendliest rivalry in the history of the sport - had begun.

My initial success changed Mother's mind. She gave me her blessing to try my hand at boxing as a career. Three weeks after the Abbott affair Ancil introduced me to the home folks in a fight with Maxie Brown in Oakland. He too went down in one. Two weeks later, in the same arena, I experienced my first extended effort. I needed five rounds to knock out Jack Petric. By the end of 1934

I had stopped Gene Garner in one at Los Angeles, Frank Ketter in one at Chicago, Johnny Baker in two at Waterloo, Iowa, Red Fields in one at Des Moines, Mickey McGoorty in one at Cleveland, Big Boy Cook in one at Kansas City, Bumbo Myer in two at Wheeling, West Virginia, Henry Surrette in one at Boston, and Gene Stanton in one at Chicago. The last seven of those fights-were only a few days apart - all in December. I said to myself, "Every day in every way, I am getting better and better."

In the meantime, Max had returned to his favorite occupation of pursuing the fair sex, too many of whom arranged to be easily caught. He was alternately in Hollywood, where Paramount Studios wanted to capitalize on his Carnera victory with a quick full-length film, and New York. If Max had been able to divide himself into three, there wouldn't have been enough of him to meet all the demands on his time or the stream of requests for personal appearances. At least 10 Maxes would have been required to maintain peace within his feminine contingent. Ronald Wagoner of United Press wrote on June 20, 1934 that Max had "established two legal departments - one to take care of managerial suits and another was the ladies auxiliary. This department is supposed to get Maxie off as cheaply as possible." Mr. Wagoner was referring to Max's following of ladies who saw in him a chance to further themselves. They were not serious about him, nor he about them. Lawsuits followed.

But there was another group of successful women who over a two-year period evinced serious interest in Max, and he in them. Among them were two New York socialites, Mary Kirk Brown and Edna Dunham; June Knight, New York musical comedy star; Betty Dumbris of the Ziegfield Follies; Alice Faye and Jean Harlow of motion picture fame.

Max never confided to me his inner thoughts and feelings about any of these ladies. I saw them together on many occasions, and sometimes joined them for dinner or a show, but the conversation was always light-hearted and bantering or about their respective careers. Max was entranced with the possibilities of carving out a new career as an actor and would gladly talk for hours about any aspect of the theater or movie making. What I know about his love life is limited to what I read in the papers.

United Press reported in May 1934 that Jean Harlow had given Max a "love bracelet." She admitted it, but Max would say only that he would marry her if that was what she wanted, provided she got a divorce from Hal G. Rosson. "I need a smart, polished running mate like her," he said. "It was love at first sight. I think we'd get along just fine."

From June to November of 1933 the gossip columnists had much to say about Max and June Knight, with whom he was seen more than *anyone else*. In late October Ms. Knight told United Press that the "romance is off. I believe that he and Dorothy Dunbar are reconciled again." If Max had been trying to patch things up with Dorothy again, he kept it a deep dark secret from me and the rest of the world.

Judith Allen helped to make the latter half of 1934 a fun time for Max, but she wasn't alone in his affections at that time. Betty Dumbris entered the picture and took over. "Max has been KO'd by cupid again, this time by Betty Dumbris, Ziegfield show girl," United Press reported. "Max is ready to walk down the aisle with her any time she can get a divorce from her estranged husband, Murray Mayor of New York ... Baer has been in and out of love almost *continuously since* he grew-up. Society women cater to him, and more than one prominent socialite in New York, Chicago and California has bid for his attention. At least one Chicago heiress plans to go to Florida to see him in a couple of exhibition bouts later this month" (January 1935).

By April of 1935 Max had fallen in love again, this time with Mary Kirk Brown, the Broadway socialite. She visited Sacramento incognito to see Max in his home setting, but was discovered by the ever-inquiring *press*. Her identity-was established by Associated Press, whose reporter immediately asked Max whether she was now his one and only. He said that he loved her and that they would be married. A month later Ms. Brown's mother said in New York that Mary and Max had become engaged. What happened to end the engagement remains for society researchers to find out, for they were not, of course, married, and indeed their infatuation with each other disappeared on the soft breezes of the oncoming summer.

While my lover brother was doing not-so-graceful swan dive out of that series of romances, among others, he was giving fits to the producers of what would have been his second full-length movie. Paramount wanted to rush an uncomplicated fight film into production immediately after Max beat Carnera and release it in time for the big Christmas season. Max objected to the simple story, saying that he was no actor and therefore needed a strong plot. Enigmatically, he wanted to play a non-boxer role, which would have required more acting experience than he had acquired.

Paramount succumbed partway, offering him the role of a dumb milkman who somehow got into boxing. The movie would be called "The Milky Way." Max accepted, but stopped production two months later because the plot needed "beefing up." Maybe Max knew what he was talking about and did the right thing, but his action doomed the picture and he alone lost a guaranteed $50,000, not to mention what Paramount must have lost. I think he should have gone ahead with it. The public didn't expect a movie featuring a champion pugilist to be a dramatic gem. But Max had grander ideas in those days. A few years later he would have seized such an opportunity.

At the peak of his championship year (early in 1935) Max was asked by a reporter to describe his dazzling wardrobe. He said he was glad to have been asked that question, because he had just completed an inventory; 80 suits, three full-dress suits, 250 neckties, 20 pairs of shoes, 24 hats, one silk high hat, and six golf outfits.

I do not doubt his accuracy, as far as he went. He also had several very good topcoats and winter jackets. But he gave much of his clothing away. I was with him one time when he picked up a hitchhiker in the California mountains and brought him to Sacramento. It was mid-winter; the hitchhiker was clad only in a threadbare sports coat and light trousers. Max gave him his own fine overcoat and enough money to last him a few days.

Max was that way all of his life. Success only enhanced his natural instinct to be generous. I have spoken of his financial contributions to our parents, who didn't really need the money and material things he showered on them. Few, however, have observed as I have his gifts of money and clothing to down and out fighters, bums on the street, poverty-stricken kids playing on vacant city lots, and countless hitch-hikers roaming the country in search of work. He was one of a kind as a human being, just as he was as a boxer.

FROM LITTLE TO BIG BROTHER

In our early youth Max and I did not compete with each other. When I was age 10 he was 15-1/2. When I was 15, he was going on 21. The age difference in those years was too great for us to be doing the same things at the same time. Sibling rivalry didn't exist because he always considered himself vastly more important and grown-up. I was his "little brother," too wet behind the ears to share the games he played and the work he did.

Of necessity, when we were living on the Livermore farm, I went with him in the family truck to pick up old baked goods at the cookie factory in Oakland. We fed them to the pigs. It took two of us to load and unload the thousands of discarded delicacies. But Max would never let me touch the wheel, even when we were parked. Driving was for men.

Since I have no memory of resenting my lowly status in Max's eyes in those days I must not have. The situation changed in my late 'teens. At 17 I was as big as Max. At 19 I was bigger - two inches taller, 20 pounds heavier. Max still considered me his "little brother." Worse, he treated me that way when I began to fight. He kept it up throughout my ring career. He continued it during our military service and on into the post-war period when we made our first and only full-length movie together, with Abbott and Costello (that classic was called "Africa Screams"). I grew to resent this state of affairs. Whenever I suggested to Max that he stop such childhood nonsense, he would laugh it off or point out that it was good "show business." He once tried to justify it in a serious way. "Look, the facts are that you were my little brother for a very long time. It's natural that I still see you that way. I was a champion of the world. You weren't. I was doing a Broadway show before you needed a shave. I'll always be five and one-half years older than you, so don't you think you should always look up to me as your big brother?"

It really-wasn't all that important to me - it was more of an irritant than an issue of consequence. Even so, I reminded him more than once that I lasted longer than he did with Joe Louis and should have won the fight, whereas he looked like a boy scout up against Chief Geronimo when he fought Joe. I knocked out Tony Galento in seven. He needed eight. I did this and that and he did less. To which he would respond, with an understanding smile and a kindly pat on my shoulder, that "when you really grow up, Buddy, you will realize how terribly you have wronged me." Verbally, he always had the upper hand.

Far more important than our long-delayed rivalry was our love and respect for each other. He reacted to my successes and defeats and pains as if they were his own and I to his. We could carry on a conversation for hours without uttering an audible word - which we frequently did on long drives from one fight city to another - because we each were in sync with the other's thinking. We lost that ability only when Max died, and sometimes I think I have it still. Do I imagine too much, or do I really hear his silent, happy communication from out there in the wherever?

At the end of 1934 I had fought 12 official bouts (as distinguished from the early exhibitions) and had won all of them by knockouts, nine in the first round, two in the second and one in the fifth. I was advertised as Max's "little brother." To give me confidence, and to help the gate, Max was in my corner for the first four imbroglios. He put on more of a show outside the ring than I did inside, leaping high whenever I landed a punch, covering up his face and crouching when I caught a good punch. I should have been more thoughtful of my brother's theatrical needs and let each fight go a little longer.

One of those affairs did go a little longer than was good for me. Jack Petric almost matched me in size and had a longer reach. It was his 40th fight, or thereabouts, and my third. In the first round he landed a powerful left hook on my right eye. Seeing the damage, he continued to pepper the eye with jabs I was unable to stop. Max screamed at me to keep my left up in front of my face. In the second I floored Jack, but he bounced up and resumed his tattoo job on my eye, which by then was as lit up as the Aura Borealis. Jack out-boxed me again in the third, but in the fourth I scored with a left-handed smash to his mid-riff. He sank slowly to the canvas and gasped loudly for air, but rose at nine and walked into another left, this time to the side of his head, and went down again. Twice more before the bell it was up and down for Jack, then the fifth and final round was seen this way by Alan Ward of the Oakland Tribune: "Petric tried to get his jab working, but Bud ignored it and pressed on for the finish. A left to the body sent Jack down for three seconds and as he rose, Bud unleashed a terrific swing that caught him flush on the side of his face. Petric's body sailed up into the air, straightened out parallel to the ring floor, and dropped heavily. He was out cold."

For the next several days I sported what Ward called the "most perfect, artistic black eye ever to evolve from pugilism." He admired the color scheme, with "blacks, blues, greens and a few touches of mauve extending from the lower lid almost to the angle of his jaw, closed as tightly as a bank vault after the office force has departed for the day." Such prose! I've always liked Alan Ward's way with the pen. He made me proud to be the owner of such a shiner.

December 1934 was one of the most memorable months of my life. I fought seven times in cities from coast to coast, including Des Moines, Wheeling, Kansas City and Boston. For a youngster like me, who had rarely been off home turf until Max won the championship, that was spectacular living. I made a lot more money than Max had done at the same stage of his career, though I never doubted that a good part of the reason was that I was Max's brother. Max received $35 for his second fight. I got 30 percent of the gate. If my name hadn't been Baer, I would have had to have fought at least 10 to 12 times to rate that much money. My relationship to Max also accounts for my quick national exposure. My record alone would not have earned me a spot on programs featuring ranked fighters in such major centers as Chicago, Kansas City and Boston. It helps to be in the right place at the right time and to have the world's heavyweight champion as your brother.

Of course, I had to be a big winner to move as fast as I did. On January 4, 1935 I extended my victory string to 13 by knocking out Jack O'Dowd in the second round. The featured fight of the night was Joe Louis, fighting in his hometown of Detroit, against Patsy Perroni. By this time, Joe had been a professional less than one year, but he had pulverized a small army of guys out of the same stables that had furnished my opponents. He was nationally recognized as a coming champion. I was not - except in the eyes of Max, who was then telling the world that I would succeed him when he retired. Joe was ranked far ahead of me because he had built a big reputation as an amateur and was well known when he turned pro. My first fight was as a pro, so I had more to learn about ring craft than he did. Even so, his professional record was no better than mine. We both specialized in early knockouts. Perroni proved an exception to the rule that night. He lasted the full 10 rounds after being decked three times.

My first defeat came six days later in Boston. Max and I were on the same program, though his was a four-round exhibition and mine was the real thing. Max turned in the funniest performance I've ever seen in the ring. A professional clown couldn't have done any better. His knees wobbled as Charlie Chaplin's did in "City Lights." He got tangled in the ropes, arms and legs flailing as he balanced on the middle strand. He avoided a blow by turning a backward somersault. Dick Madden, his opponent, gave up trying to be serious and joined the audience in laughter. He was good enough that even the newspaper critics applauded at ringside and the next day praised rather than damned him for playing the fool.

But I took a drubbing when I faced Babe Hunt, whom Max had toyed with a week earlier in Detroit. Babe could box with the best. He couldn't hit hard, but he hit often. As a dancer he was Fred Astaire. He used his speed and agility to stay out of my range and to score points with a flicking left jab and an occasional powder-puff right. At the end, only my pride was damaged. I had lost every round by a wide margin, without feeling a single punch to my head or body. It should be known, however, that some of Babe's punches were illegal gouges with the thumb of his glove. I responded with an illegal butt and was caught by the referee. Even if I had done a better job of boxing, the butt would have cost me the fight.

By this time there had been a spate of articles in the press dealing with the possibility that Max and I might wind up in the same ring. Typical of the speculation was this item by Ronald Wagoner for United Press: "Max says that he intends to keep the title for 10 years and pass it on to Buddy. Will two brothers meet in the ring for the first time in history to fight for the heavyweight crown? Some ringsiders say such a battle would be a frame-up or a hoax. Others say it is possible. They point out that no man in the world likes to be whipped by his kid brother and, by the same token, any man in the world would appreciate nothing more than to beat an older brother, for marbles or money or just for fun. The brothers Baer already get a little rough with each other when they spar."

I have a hard time remembering exactly how I thought about it at the time, probably because I didn't want to think about it at the time. I recall quite clearly that I didn't see who could beat Max in the foreseeable future. At the same time I was personally confident that I would rise to the position of No. 1 challenger. If Max continued to be champion, and I gained top ranking as challenger, would a match between us be avoidable? Wouldn't we be forced to fight each other? This is where my memory breaks down. I assume that I found comfort in the idea that Max would retire as champion, and that I would fight other contenders in an elimination tournament for the crown. As it turned out, I'm grateful that a match between us was never needed.

Boston is a beautiful city and a great fight town. It also ranks as one of the coldest inhabited places on the planet in January, so Max and I were pleased to board a southbound train and watch the snow and ice slowly disappear as we sped toward Tampa, Florida. The tropical breezes brought out the best in me - a right to the head of Marty Hogan, from which he was unable to rise in the first round, and a combination to the jaw of Tommy Davenport over in Miami, giving me another one-round kayo. Max fought two exhibitions with local heroes, who were allowed to hit Max every now and then without serious retaliation. Max used the occasions to demonstrate his rubber legs act, to the great amusement of the fans. I began to wonder if this fooling around had not gone on too long, that Max might be hurting for lack of real action.

We stayed in Miami for most of February, soaking up the sun and enjoying our notoriety as we gamboled on the beach, drawing awed stares from physically less endowed men and provocative gazes from physically better endowed women. Perhaps some of the bathing beauties had read recent reports that I had never been kissed by anyone other than my mother (or Max, who usually planted a loud buss on my cheek after my every win). It was said that I was too shy to even talk to a girl. Maybe some of the lasses were thinking I needed lessons. It was hard to avoid such speculation, for I was neither blind nor deaf and I could see and hear the invitations framed on the lips of one gorgeous creature after another. Max called me dumb not to respond. He himself needed no invitations, though he got them. Advanced on the pulchritude of Miami Beach as if he were back in a Broadway chorus line. We started each day together, but finished it separately - he with beautiful company, me with my shadow. Dumb. I was dumb beyond any more words on the subject.

Then it was back to Oakland and a match that was being advertised as the first true test of my career. Frank Connelly was almost my size. He had ruled the amateurs for four years and was cold-cocking the pros with ease. He announced that I would serve as an important stepping stone on his way to the top. When the first round began he touched me lightly with a left jab; I countered with a left feint and brought a roundhouse right, with all of my power, to the point of his jaw. I knew that he would not rise at nine, but when he failed to recover in two or three minutes I became alarmed. Max rushed into the ring and pushed Connelly's handler's aside. They were trying to raise him to a sitting position, and his ears were turning white. Max yelled that they were killing him. Instead, he raised his legs to force the blood into his brain. It worked. A few writers said that Max had probably saved Connelly's life. The house doctor agreed.

It was at about this time that voices - other than Max's, that is began to be heard in the land suggesting that maybe I was in the top several challengers for the crown. Writers on both coasts said that after my easy win over Connelly I could no longer be brushed aside as a brash upstart. Aside from Louis, the main contenders were Primo Carnera, Max Schmeling, Steve Hamas, Ray Impellitierre and Art Lasky. By the end of March, Schmeling had knocked out Hamas and Carnera had eliminated Impellitierre. Lasky was to be tested by an in and out old timer by the name of James J. Braddock. And then there was me.

Ancil Hoffman figured that I could whip Carnera without any further experience. Most of the writers agreed. But Primo wouldn't give me a bout, on grounds that he was entitled to a return match with Max. Ancil thought I needed more experience before tangling with a skilled boxer such as Lasky. As for Joe, I would need a lot more of everything before risking my career with him.

Max and I then took off for Grand Rapids, Michigan, where he was to fight another exhibition pending a decision on his opponent for a June title defense and I would face Harry Nelson. I knocked out my man in three, Max put on another comedy routine, and back in Madison Square Garden Jimmy Braddock scored a convincing upset over Art Lasky. The Garden, which had to exercise its legal right to stage a title fight by June, looked with favor on Mr. Braddock.

Money, not logic, was the main factor in deciding who would fight Max. Schmeling had earned the right, but he wanted to hold the match in Europe, where taxes (when combined with the U.S. levy) would amount to more than Max's share of the gate. Louis had yet to meet Carnera or Schmeling, so he would have to wait his turn. Braddock became the Garden's choice. My brother happily agreed, for he liked Jimmy personally and also felt that he would give him little trouble in the ring. We both departed Grand Rapids for Chicago, he to start training for Braddock, and I to fight the man who launched Braddock on the comeback trail Corn Griffith. Griffith had been knocked out by Braddock in a preliminary to Max's title fight with Carnera. I felt I had to do as well, and I did. Corn went down in two. He lasted three with Braddock.

Max and I had ended our series of appearances in the same ring. He would come to Buffalo in May to watch me destroy Big Boy Brackey, but he would not fight again until he faced Braddock the following month. His presence in Buffalo, however, helped to raise the stature of my fight well beyond what it deserved. Big Boy was touted as the toughest human being to emerge from Buffalo since a native son survived going over Niagara Falls in a barrel back in 1910. He had knocked out a long string of opponents and bragged that I would make an attractive addition to his list. I had never seen as much advance publicity for a fight of mine. It should have scared me, but it didn't. Frank Pacassi, my own advance man and No. 1 trainer, showed his confidence in me by betting Brackey's manager, Tom Timlin, that I would win without being knocked down. He picked up $50 when I pounded Big Boy to the deck seven times in the first minute and 40 seconds, ending the fight with a K.O. Not only did I stay on my feet, I ducked the only real punch Brackey was able to throw.

The encounter with Big Boy was a watershed event for me, being the last time I would ever fight as the brother - big or little - of the world's heavyweight champion. Max defended his title on June 13, an unlucky number, in the Madison Square

Garden Bowl on Long Island, a place where no champion had ever successfully defended his title. He lost.

It appeared obvious that Max had frittered away his crown long before the 15th and final round ended. He had been penalized two rounds for low blows and another for wrestling. Braddock had outboxed him in at least eight of the other rounds. Max's only chance was to knock him out, and it looked as though he had lost the power to do that. I vaulted into the ring and hugged Max as soon as the announcer, Al Frazin, got out these words, "the winner, and new champion..." I could see that he was near tears, and so was I, for I never doubted that Max was the better fighter and that what had happened was a tragedy not only for Max and our family but for boxing. It is not good for boxing when a clearly superior fighter somehow contrives to lose a title match, even when he deserves to lose, as Max did that night. On this occasion, the saving grace for the sport was Jimmy Braddock himself - one of the nicest guys ever to put on gloves.

Just a few weeks before the big fight Jimmy was so broke that he had to accept relief to feed his three kids. He grew up poor, a product of New York's 10th Avenue, where you have to be tough to survive childhood. He worked a few days a month as a longshoreman and tried to make ends meet by fighting. All of his purses had been small - too small to meet family needs. When he stepped into the ring to meet Max, he had lost 20 of 80 fights, was a 10 to 1 underdog, but was determined not to blow this opportunity to achieve financial solvency. When the bell for round one sounded, he was as perfect a picture of human resoluteness as I have ever seen. Max wore a sappy smile, as if he were telling the fans that he was wasting his time with a has-been but would take care of him at his pleasure.

Jimmy kept Max at bay for the first three rounds while scoring solid left jabs to Max's head, with several jolting rights thrown in. Max behaved as if he didn't understand that this fight was for his title. He had to show off his rubber legs and mugging ability, as in so many of his exhibitions. The crowd accepted his hamming in the sure knowledge that Max would lower the boom whenever he chose to do so.

In the fourth round Max began to wake up and force the action himself. He slammed Jimmy into the ropes with a left hook. It looked as though Jimmy's time might have come, but no, he rallied and bounced a right off Max's chin. Max shook his head and stared at his left hand. Thereafter he used his left mainly for slapping or feinting. He thought it was broken.

Max was the clear aggressor in the fifth but lost the round for a backhand punch. He also lost the effective use of his right hand for the rest of the fight when he glanced a blow off Jimmy's shoulder, fracturing his wrist. Though the fans didn't know it, the battle was as good as over. After the fight, Max was roundly criticized for what one writer called "the lousiest performance in the history of heavyweight title fights." I strongly disagree. I think it was a gutty performance. He fought the last 10 rounds without the only weapons a fighter is permitted to use. A blow with either hand gave him intense pain, yet he rained enough punches on James J. Braddock to win several of those rounds. The fact that he could not get any steam into the punches should have been understandable to the critics. I will concede only that Max was not mentally prepared for such a tenacious opponent as Braddock turned out to be that night. I still believe that had he not broken his right hand, he would have recovered his poise in time to knock Jimmy out.

Max lost his heavyweight crown in June, 1935, but this photo of one of his trips back to Livermore, suggested that his hometown fans were confident he would be back.

Max was a good sport about his loss, right from the start. As I was helping him out of the ring he told reporters that Jimmy was very tough but that he would beat him in a future fight. In the dressing room he explained about his broken hands, and at the same time pointed out that such breaks can go either way and that it could have happened to Braddock. He admitted that he took Braddock too lightly, and praised Braddock's battle plan and tenacity. He never fought for the title again, of course, but he remained a respected challenger for several years to come.

Two weeks after the fight, when his hands had healed, Max and Mary Ellen Sullivan were married. Mary Ellen Sullivan? What happened to Mary Kirk Brown and Jean Harlow and all the others? All I know is that Max had met Mary a year earlier while he was in Washington, D.C., where she was manager of the coffee shop in the Willard Hotel. He told me how attractive and intelligent she was, but I paid little attention because he said that about so many. My ears perked up slightly two months before the marriage when he talked on and on about how nice she was, in addition to all of her other virtues. But I was in no way prepared for his marriage especially the way it happened. I had just knocked out Frank Wotanski in the first round at Yankee Stadium (it was the semi-final preliminary to the Louis-Carnera fight). I mentioned casually to Max that Wotanski was a native of Utica, New York, and asked, "Isn't that Mary Sullivan's home town?" He nodded, congratulated me on the win, and said he had to leave immediately for Washington, D.C. Two days later he and Mary tied the knot.

I read that the Willard Hotel management was furious with Max. It seems that he proposed to

Mary in the morning, she resigned on the spot, and they were married in the afternoon. "It wasn't fair to the hotel," the manager was quoted as saying. "She should have given me time to find a replacement, and Max with his experience in the world should have insisted on it." Max responded that all is fair in love and war. Could such a marriage last? It truly was made in heaven. Max settled down to become a family man, and loved it. Mary was devoted to him and their children, and seemed blissfully happy as long as he lived some 24 years following their wedding.

I recovered quickly from the shock of Max's sudden romantic leap and turned to the business at hand - climbing the fistic ladder. Ancil predicted that my July 18 fight with Al Delaney in Buffalo would be my hardest test yet. Delaney, I was told, hit like a trip-hammer and could take it. He was only 19, a year younger than me, but had already caught the eye of matchmakers in New York. (The matchmakers remembered that Al had bopped Joe Louis around the ring in their amateur days.)

The advance reports were true. Delaney landed the most stunning blow I had ever received. I was in the fog for at least a minute. I remember nothing about what I did in that time. I must have kept out of his way by instinct. The punch dropped me to one knee, making it the first knockdown I had ever suffered. That was in the first round. In the second I decked Al twice, but in the process landed low. The round was taken away from me, so I was behind two rounds to none in a four-round battle (as minors we weren't allowed to go more than four). In the third I scored three knockdowns and asked the referee to stop it before Al got hurt. He waved me back to battle as the bell sounded. I knocked him cold in the first minute of the fourth. I felt like criticizing the referee for letting it go that far, but remembered my "minor" status and held my tongue.

"Buddy Now Big Brother Baer?" was the headline in one of the papers the next day. I mailed it to Max at his honeymoon retreat.

PROFESSIONAL PROTECTION

Lord knows I am old enough (I will be 67 in May, 1983) to understand that the underworld and the world of boxing are not unknown to each other. Yet I pranced happily through my boxing career (as did Max), at a time when gangsterism was in flower, without ever feeling the scratch of a mobster's claw. Max was more worldly than I, but we both were heavyweight innocents in the land of Beelzebub.

Neither of us was ever involved in a crooked fight. We were never asked to do anything shady. Nor were we even witness to a fight we suspected might be less than honest. But such things were going on around us. Some boxers did take dives for gamblers. Some managers did sacrifice their fighters, for a price. Some referees did do as they were told, to keep their jobs. Some promoters did swindle the boxers who made their programs possible. I know, because we read about such things, or were told about them. We didn't see them ourselves because we wore the very best of rose colored glasses.

It didn't occur to us that when the Capone gang gave us unsolicited protection against threats of serious bodily harm that we were about as close to the underworld as one could get in 1935. The incident started while we were in Miami Beach. Ralph Capone, brother of Al, came to our hotel room to ask a favor. Al's son was in the hospital recovering from head injuries sustained when he fainted in church and hit his temple on a corner of the pew. Al wondered if we would be kind enough to pay him a visit. The kid looked up to us as heroes. We readily agreed, and spent an hour with young Capone. That was all, but Capone, Sr., didn't cease expressing his appreciation until he disappeared behind prison walls -convicted of income tax fraud.

The first such expression came a few days later in Capone's hometown of Chicago. Ancil stayed in a hotel room adjoining ours. About 10 o'clock that evening we heard loud shouts in his room, followed by the sound of shattering glass. We rushed in and found two guys trying to push Ancil out the window - 23 floors up. Max grabbed one, I grabbed the other, and Ancil pulled himself back into the safety of the room. I was getting ready to call the house police when there was a loud banging on Ancil's door. It turned out to be a representative of "Mr. Capone," who apologized for being late. It seems that an hour or so earlier one of the gang had overheard a restaurant conversation between two men who were planning to take Ancil's contract with Max away from him - by force if necessary. Al heard about it and immediately sent one of his men to protect Ancil.

We were treated to the sight of a Capone man calling the police to pick up what he called "a couple of hoods." We laughed about that for years after, supposing that we might have been in on an historical first: Capone calling the cops. After the cops took the hoods away, Capone's man said he had been instructed to stay with us the rest of the night. He sat in a chair outside Ancil's door until we left the next morning. Ancil later testified that he had never heard of the two hooligans who knocked on his door, that he had let them in, that they offered him $100,000 for Max's contract, that he had expressed surprise and outrage, and was then pushed into the window and nearly out of it. What they would have gained by killing Ancil remained undetermined. I don't know to this day, and in any event we never heard about the case again.

We were often in Chicago, if for no other reason than to change trains. In those days it was not possible to travel from coast to coast on the mid-America route without going through, and changing trains in, the Windy City. Somehow, Capone always knew when we were there, and provided us a cab and the protection of his gang as long as we stayed. "Protection" meant following us when we went about the city, and watching our hotel rooms at night.

It was like waiting for the other shoe to drop. We didn't know what we were being protected from. We didn't savor being tailed by Capone, or seeing a Capone man patrolling our hotel corridor. We had told these guys, over and over, that we didn't need their services. They said they had their orders. We tried to ignore them, expecting to learn at any time the reason for all this attention. What did Capone want from us? The answer to that question wasn't pleasant to consider.

The answer came one day in May. Ralph called to ask if we were okay. "Just fine," I answered. "And would you mind telling us why you are so thoughtful about our welfare?" "I'm very surprised," Ralph said. "I thought you understood all along that Al is just trying to thank you for being so good to his son. He doesn't forget things like that, and neither do I." So our worst fear - that someone in the gang might wish to rearrange a fight, forcing us to deny the request and risk the kind of peril for which the Capones were famous - never materialized. Al Capone was being sentimental.

If there had been no gangsters in the 'thirties, fights would still have been fixed. Some managers and some promoters didn't need the help of organized crime to execute devious maneuvers of their own. Consider the case of Nate Lewis, manager of Harry Thomas, and Joe Jacobs, manager of Max Schmeling and Tony Galento.

I was in Des Moines, Iowa on October 30, 1939 to fight Lee Savold when the Des Moines Register came out with a front page filled with stories about Thomas admitting to "fake fights with Schmeling and Galento." Thomas made his confession to Arch Ward of the Chicago Tribune, who said Thomas had agreed to take a dive against Schmeling on December 13, 1937 and against Galento on November 14, 1938 - in both cases at the urging of Nate Lewis and with the connivance of Joe Jacobs. The purpose of the fixes, Thomas

Professional protection / 165

told Ward, was to build up the reputations of challengers for Joe Louis' title.

Thomas spelled out in detail how each fix was accomplished, who said what to whom, and the difficulties he experienced in trying to make his dives look legitimate. Jacobs and Lewis denied everything, and eventually escaped without penalty or censure. I believe Thomas told the truth.

The cloud of that odoriferous story hung over me that night as I battled Savold. I simply couldn't concentrate for thinking of it, and of what the fans might be thinking of us. Would all of us be suspect?

I won in eight rounds, by decision, and was pleased to find that both the press and the fans thought we had performed very well. I quickly forgot about gangsters and fixes and crooked managers. Max and Ancil and I were too busy trying to profit by doing our best to even think about doing our worst for profit. I think that most other fighters and managers, then and now, are the same.

One of Max's several hotshot cars is the backdrop for this photo of Buddy and Max's wife, Mary, around 1937.

Max's second and last marriage to Mary Ellen Sullivan, turned him from a gay lothario into a family man. This 1946 picture shows the couple with their children, Maudie, Max, Jr., and Jimmie. A ham to the end, Max demonstrates the fine art of fly-casting.

I BELIEVE

Joe Louis, at the peak of his form, was probably the most efficient, devastating and coolly ruthless fighter in the history of boxing. The difference between Joe at his best and all the rest was the power of his two-handed attack. He was lethal with both right and left, either of which generated stunning force from a distance of a mere 10 or 12 inches from his target. He wasted few punches. A steady forward mover, he jabbed with lightning fast stabs, jolting his victims into fatal defensive mistakes, then moved in with triphammer blows that usually spelled the end of the fight. He couldn't take a hard punch as well as some - Tommy Farr, for example - but he rallied well and had loads of courage. He was, in fact, most dangerous immediately after a rare knockdown or a telling blow to his head. He roared back with a kind of ferocity the likes of which the ring had never seen -totally controlled, relentless, overwhelming.

Joe was at his best on the night of September 24, 1935, when he fought Max at Yankee Stadium. He wasn't angry - as he was for his second fight with Schmeling - just determined. Determined and incredibly disciplined. He knew exactly what he wanted to do, and followed his plan without deviation from the opening bell. Paul Gallico, one of the best of the sportswriters, called it an execution."

Max was as prepared for this fight as for any battle of his career. For six weeks he had adhered to a rigid training schedule, faithfully following every routine established by Ancil and his trainers. He too was determined. He had more to be determined about than did Louis, for just three months earlier he had, to use his words, "thrown away" his title. He had been humiliated. It was extremely important to Max the man that he regain his dignity. " I've got to win, for Mom and Pop, for Mary and Buddy-I've got to win for myself."

Joe scored a psychological triumph two hours before the fight began. He married Marva Trotter in the early evening, and after the ceremony said his wedding present would be a victory over Max. When Max married Dorothy Dunbar, he waited until after his fight with Paulino Uzcudun, and lost the fight by protecting his handsome mug "for Dorothy." The implications of Joe's pre-fight wedding were not lost on Max.

The fight was more than just another gladiatorial contest. The winner had been promised an opportunity to meet Braddock for the championship. Max felt certain that he would beat Braddock in a return match. So did most of the fight fans of America and the world for whom Max was still Numero Uno despite his antics over the years. All he had to do was get by Louis, and Joe by then was regarded by many professional scribes as the uncrowned champion. So two determined men moved out to meet each other when the bell sounded for the first round.

I was at ringside, dressed and ready to fight Ford Smith in a later match. Max flicked a left into Joe's face. Joe fired back with a two-handed barrage to Max's body. I saw the pain. I felt the pain. I was Max. I cried out advice, "keep your guard up!" Too late. Joe found an opening to Max's chin. He spun around. I felt faint. Max pushed him away, cocked his right, and staggered backward from a left to the side of his head. He managed to stay out of range until the bell, and wobbled to his corner.

Max did better in the second round. He landed several body smashes, and finally, just before the round ended, scored with a vicious right to Joe's mouth. But he had taken 40 to 50 blows while meting out about 10. Before the third round began, Jack Dempsey, Max's second, told Max to "keep it up, he hasn't laid a glove on you." To which Max responded, as he moved out for the third round, "then you better watch the referee, somebody's beating the hell out of me!"

Round three was an unrelieved disaster for Max. I estimated that he took around 210 punches to various parts of his head and gave virtually nothing back. He went down twice. The first knockdown was also the first of his career. He rose and advanced into a new barrage that decked him until the bell sounded at the count of four. Never in his career had he taken such a beating, and he never would again. (Lou Nova cut him up badly four years later, but Nova had no pizzazz. He would have needed the power of both hands and both feet to match a casually thrown Louis punch.) The end came toward the end of round four when Max was slammed to the canvas for the third time. He pulled himself up to one knee and waited for the 10-count. A roar of boos filled the night air. Had he quit, as the crowd most assuredly thought?

Of course, no one would expect me to agree with that verdict, and I not only disagree, I disagree passionately. Max was thoroughly beaten. He had been battered by hundreds of murderous smashes to his head and body. His right hand had again been hurt, this time in the first round. Dempsey said immediately after the fight that he thought it was broken. It turned out to be a bad sprain. So again he was without his primary weapon. Few if any fighters of the time could have absorbed the blows that Max took. Louis himself said immediately after the fight that he had never seen such a "tough chin." "Never hit a man like I hit ol Max Baer," he commented later. "Every time I did, it was like driving a brick out of a wall." That Max refused to rise and take a final - possibly disastrous series of rights and lefts when he was defenseless, says more of his good sense than his courage. He had already, in very large measure, demonstrated his fortitude.

Max's fate so bothered me that when my turn came I performed as an automaton rather than as Buddy Baer. I was sick, and I couldn't rid my mind of the sight that had me sick. Visions of Max being bludgeoned around the ring loomed larger than the vision of my opponent, Ford Smith, who I should have whipped- with ease. Instead, I lost - and deserved to lose - a six round decision.

I believe that Max at his best had enough right hand power to knock out Joe Louis at his best. I believe that I also had that kind of power. What neither of us had was similar power in our left hands, and, more importantly, the burning desire to be fighters - sometimes called the "killer instinct." Joe had both of those qualities, in abundance.

In his dressing room, after the Louis fight, Max stated his own case. "I never wanted to fight. I never was cut out to be a fighter, and I shouldn't have been in the ring tonight. I'm through." The fact that he decided to continue fighting doesn't alter his candid opinion of himself.

Jimmy Braddock, some years after his retirement, told Peter Heller in an interview for Heller's book, "In This Corner," that Max was "a dynamite puncher. If he hit you right, he'd knock you out in the third row. In my opinion the guy was a harder puncher than Louis. Louis was a faster puncher and he hit you with more punches, but Baer was a guy who could hurt you ... He was a nice fellow but he should never have been a fighter. His ability was, if the guy could have got mad, you know, like guys get in a fight, he'd kill you with a punch, because he had killed a couple of guys, and I think that was on his mind. But I always said that Max should have been an actor instead of a fighter."

My case was substantially different from Max's. I became a fighter because he had made a success of fighting, and because I had the physical equipment to make my decision seem like following the path Mother Nature had laid out for me. I was serious about boxing. Max was not. I was of the school of "art for art's sake" - I wanted to win for the sake of winning. Max was attracted more to the sideshow that always accompanies successful heavyweights, and because he himself was a master showman, he converted the sideshow into the main show. But I was the same as Max in the one critical area that determines ultimate achievement in the ring - especially in an era when the competition was tough and plentiful. I lacked the needed amount of desire to climb the highest fistic mountains of my time. Mother Nature failed to give me a killer instinct to go along with my physique.

Bob Considine, another of the fine sports writers of the period, used the event of my loss to Gunnar Barlund (I will go into that fight later) to dissect my personality as a fighter. His column was perceptive, but flawed. The following is a substantial excerpt:

"He became a fighter because his brother was a fighter. From his brother he picked up all that curious lack of will-to-win which made Max forfeit hundreds of thousands of dollars which would have come to him if he had had an ounce or two more competitive fury in his system. Max couldn't get up enough interest while fighting Jim Braddock to throw the punches that would have saved his title. Buddy, with just as much native talent going to waste, was equally unmoved by the absurdity of standing with his hands at his side and letting Barland slap him into tears.

"Buddy was never meant to fight. He was born to be the adoring younger brother of a quick-thinking, successful, bantering elder. Somehow we feel that the happiest moment of his life was the night Max beat Primo Carnera for the heavyweight title. There was a victory party after that fight at Dempsey's (Jack's restaurant in New York). And Buddy, flushed with the effects of two Coca-colas and the thrill of seeing his brother-hero triumph, stood up at the end of the crowded dining room and, sang 'Cocktails for Two' in his boyish baritone. All he wanted to be that night was the champ's brother.

"But there was no way he could escape being a fighter. His very size and shape made it inevitable ... So Buddy became a fighter, and Heaven had lavished such an abundance of physical gifts on him that he was a winning fighter. But as the unpredictable Max began to fritter away one golden opportunity after another, Buddy descended with him. The night Max resigned to Louis, Buddy, minus what precious little stomach he has for the game, was soundly beaten by Ford Smith.

"If there were some way in which the heart and gall and rankling ire of Tony Galento could be grafted on to the wondrous hide of Buddy Baer, Baer would wade through the heavyweight picture like a tornado and make short work of Joe Louis. For no man could stop that combination of supernatural brawn and hitting power plus the driving force of Tony's tub-sized ticker.

"Long since, Buddy Baer should have become the first brother of a heavyweight champion to win the title. But Nature is hard to budge. Nature, thumbing through the pages of life, chose a different role for him. When it gave him his vast strength and his muscular fluency, it meant him to use it on a farm or in some other placid work. Circumstances forced him to go against Nature, to try to improve upon his preordained role. But Nature, we suspect, will have the last laugh."

I cringe at some of his language, but I concede that he was right about this: I lacked the determination to accept any measure of punishment in order to inflict whatever amount of punishment might be necessary to win, regardless of the consequences to myself or to my opponent. Mother Nature did not give me that kind of instinct. Mother Baer did not raise her son to be a butcher of human beings. I am happy on both counts.

But I don't think I needed either quality to have been a champion. I said at the start of these pages that I think I should have won the first Louis fight. That would have made me the champion. I think that the championship would have improved my outlook and self-confidence. Perhaps my primary weaknesses - relative slowness afoot and insufficient left handed authority - would have been overcome by new determination born of a champion's confidence. I would have been equipped to defend my title successfully, I think - against Louis or Schmeling or anyone else around at that time. I wouldn't have been a killer tornado, but I would have been a good champion.

As for my behavior at Max's championship party, Considine failed to point out that I was 18 at the time, I had not yet decided to become a fighter, and my "boyish baritone" was good enough to elicit suggestions from responsible people that I consider a singing career. But the occasion was surely the happiest moment of my life up to that time.

THE BARITONE AFFAIR

I learned a long time ago that within every sportswriter lurks a Ring Lardner, a Wodehouse, and a Bob Hope, straining to be revealed. Humor is their forte. Boxers and baseball players are their favorite subjects. The result can be a typographical comedy that runs a full page in length before telling who won. The urge to be creative and funny can overpower the need to report.

I was exposed to my share of sports page witticisms, even though I was not as colorful as Brother Max, Tony Galento, Kingfish Levinsky or Mohammed Ali, among a host of others, who really earned the ribbing they took. But color is not a requirement to be the lead funnyman in a sports story. Ineptness will do quite well for most writers. A mashed nose and cauliflower ears are excellent comic material as is body shape - too tall, too short, too squat, too fat, too lean. Any boxer unfortunate enough to play a musical instrument - particularly a violin or the drums would become the Paganini of Pugilism or a Bomber Beethoven in the hands of the writers. In my case, when the writers tired of parodying my size, or my dazzling footwork, or my preference for soft drinks, they fell back on my voice. Imagine their glee when I was signed to fight another baritone, Jack Doyle of Ireland.

"Caroling Cuffers All Doyle had all the requirements for a royal roast. He was Hollywood handsome, 204 pounds of matinee idol, champion of Irish heavyweights, husband of movie star Judith Allen, and he had played in several film shorts - not as a boxer, mind you, but as a singer. I had sung only at small social gatherings, but the writers knew I could carry a tune, and promptly labeled the match the "Battle of the Baritones."

Set to Show Dancers Some Real Art," ran a top-of-the-page headline in the New York Post of August 29, 1935. The story, by Jack Buck, explained: "The dance is an art, as was demonstrated last night at Madison Square Garden. (A dancing contest had been held.) What can be done with song remains an uncertainty, at least until tonight when Buddy Baer and Jack Doyle are presented in a novelty number with boxing gloves.

"Doyle is a baritone of the old school, a singer of Irish ballads. Max Baer's brother Buddy is also a baritone, but he goes in for modern music -jazz. There is really little to choose, as each so far has succeeded in remaining on his feet.

"The song will be on their lips but not in their hearts ... as both Doyle and Buddy have promised to express themselves with boxing gloves in the garden ring ... There was dancing in the Garden last night and this evening there will be some song, and perhaps some fighting."

A multi-panel cartoon ran under the story. One panel had one of us singing "TANKS for the Buggy Ride," while the other took a dive. That was called the "Theme Song." In the "Overture" I was banging away at Doyle's head while singing, "My head is bloody but unbowed, SING IT!" To which Doyle said, "I don't seem to recall the words." A panel titled "Bass Note" showed one of us singing "Sweet and Low" while the other rolled on the floor yelling "Foul!" In "Requiem" the referee was playing the piano; one of us was singing "One - two -three - four - sometimes I wisht there wuz more, and as the other from his prone position called out, "Sing it slow!"

Doyle was known as the "Irish Nightingale," and "Irish Thrush," the "Irish Harp," or just "The Harp." For this battle I was variously called the "Bully Baritone" (a reference to the abattoir in my past), the "Crooning Cruncher" or "Jazzing Jacob."

Paul Gallico, writing in the New York Daily News, chose to satirize our manliness rather than our tonsils. "Is there no one who will step in and stop this thing before it is too late?" he began his piece. "Yes, I am referring to the proposed brutal slugging match scheduled in New York's blood drenched arena...between Buddy Baer, the Western Pithecanthrope, and Jack Doyle, the Giant of the Trogh-na-dayr, the largest man whose stamp of foot ever set the Irish hills to shaking; Doyle, the minstrel boy with the voice of an angel; the counterpart of Lugh the Terrible. Oh, God help us all, this thing has gone too far, and unless wiser heads prevail there will be a slaughter in the city tonight, for those two mighty men cannot face one another at grips without death being the victor."

Every paper in New York was filled with similar flights of fancy. Much of the stuff was syndicated across the nation By the time Doyle and I squared off to fight I'm not sure that either of us was certain whether we should sing, waltz, pull out the corner posts or engage in fisticuffs. The referee straightened us out on that point, and Doyle promptly nailed me on the left eye with a solid right. I swung, wildly, and hit him on the thigh. He went down, clutched his midriff and looked at the referee for an indication of a foul but got no response. We exchanged a flurry of rights and lefts, one of which - mine - knocked Doyle off his feet again. He bounced up and I drove him into a corner and dropped him a third time. I thought he was down for keeps, but at the count of five he pulled himself up and walked right into my best-left hook. Stunned, he stared blankly at the crowd. I moved in to throw a right, and the referee stopped it. Time: 2:38 minutes of the first round.

If I hadn't TKO'd him, I would have lost the round because of the low blow. Doyle complained that the blow cost him the fight because it made him ill. It was the first time I had ever heard of a punch to the thigh (I didn't mean to hit him there, of course) inducing nausea. His wife, Judith Allen, fainted at ringside when the referee stopped the fight, and had to be carried out on a stretcher. "The match proved Doyle's courage but it also proved he cannot fight," concluded Bill Farnsworth, Jr. of the <u>New York Journal American.</u>

THE YEAR THAT WASN'T

1936 was a great year for Roosevelt - he carried every state except Maine and Vermont in winning re-election by the greatest margin in history. Clark Gable continued to mint money in Hollywood, and "The Great Ziegfield" won the Academy Award for best picture. It was a bad year for Haile Selassie, who escaped Ethiopia on a British warship as Mussolini announced the annexation of his country. Hitler took over the Rhineland and the Spanish civil war began, making it a bad year for peace. I wasn't paying much attention to any of those events, but somehow the mood of impending disaster seeped into my veins and arteries. I became lethargic, like a hound in the dog days of August and managed to lose an important fight with Andre Lenglet, heavyweight champion of France.

I was supposed to win. Odds favored me, 13 to 10. But writers asked me several times as fight day (April 22) approached if I was feeling O.K. They said I looked terrible in workouts. Was anything bothering me? I couldn't think of one reason to be upset or worried. Our family was in good health. I was not suffering from lack of nourishment. I had knocked out Jack Petric and Wally Hunt in one and beaten Millionaire Murphy in four to start off the year, so my occupational interests were being well served. Yet I had no energy. I could have napped all-day and snored all night. Ancil said it would pass. It didn't - at least in time to save me from Mr. Lenglet.

The fight was one of a kind in my experience. I nailed Andre with a combination to the jaw in the first round that sent him hurtling into the ropes. I watched as he hung on, instead of going after him for the coup de grace. He appreciated my extreme courtesy, thinking no doubt it was part of his welcome to Oakland, and stayed away from me until the bell. In the second he discovered that my inaction in the first round was not courtesy, but lethargy, and proceeded to play chopsticks on my jaw. For variation, since I didn't respond, he worked over my body with an impassioned sonata for the left hand. I let him get away with it because I was winded; yet I hadn't done anything much except to absorb his jabs. Strange. I don't understand it to this day.

Lenglet's confidence grew in the second and third rounds as he continued to have his way. He seemed as dumbfounded over my performance as I was myself, and I could see him gesticulating in his corner, between rounds, waving his gloves in my direction and seeming to ask what the hell was going on. But he got too cocky in the fifth and waded into me as if I was a punching bag and he didn't need a defense. A sudden surge of anger, or energy - I'm not sure which - poured through my lifeless frame. I stepped back and aimed a left to his jaw, then a right, then a series of lefts and rights. Blood spurted from his mouth and the corner of one eye. He staggered sideways, then backward, and I thought that maybe I had rescued myself from certain defeat. I waited for him to collapse. He didn't, and I kept thinking, "what's wrong? He should be on his back." All that thinking allowed him to recover again, and he danced and jabbed the rest of the fight, easily winning a six-round decision.

I was just as lethargic about the defeat as I had been during the fight. I told reporters that I would chalk it up to experience. They insisted that I tell them what my problem was. They had never seen me or anyone else fight like that. I seemed to be in a dream, they said. I agreed that that was the way I felt, but assured them I would get over it. Ancil said he would take me to his farm in Fair Oaks for a rest cure. I burst into song, "Swinging in a Hammock," and the puzzled press departed.

I have since been told by doctors that my trouble probably was nothing more than "growing pains." I was still inching upward and putting on weight, and my pace had been hectic. The combination of travel, fighting and growing had used up my reserve energy, I was told. Whether or not they knew what they were talking about, I did soon recover. By the end of the year I had knocked out six more opponents and decisioned one in six rounds.

All of this time - the entire year of 1936 - Max was devoting himself to the pursuit of money. He fought 18 exhibitions in such places as Twin Falls, Vancouver, Toronto, Tulsa, Boise, Dallas, Oklahoma City, Portland, Provo, Cheyenne, Platteville,

Lewiston, Ogden, San Antonio, Salt Lake City, Des Moines, Evansville and Coeur D'Alene. I joined in six of his fight programs, giving the fans two Baers for the price of one. My matches, however, were not exhibitions, but rather stepping stones toward the top. Max was simply marking time.

Most fight fans, even avid ones, are not aware that Max needed nearly two years to get his hands in shape for real fighting. The metacarpal bone in his right hand had been broken in the Louis fight. His left hand was full of small fractures, and the wrist had been severly sprained. By the time he began the exhibitions, nearly nine months had elapsed since the damage was incurred, and he felt able to put on a reasonably good show. He did, but without fireworks. No hard smashes by either hand. He knocked out 14 opponents with blows that wouldn't have fazed a Galento or a Schmeling.

THE BATTLES OF BRITAIN

The eyes of Britain were upon us when the sun came up on the first day of the year 1937. More precisely, the eyes belonged to Brigadier General A. C. Critchley, retired from His Majesty's Service but very much active in sponsoring boxing matches, horse races and assorted entertainment extravaganzas. In fact, he owned Harringay Arena in London, several tracks for horses and Greyhounds, and a batch of hotels in London and other British cities. He was a multi-millionaire.

Critchley had tried to arrange a return bout for Max with Joe Louis in 1936, to be staged in London, but for a variety of reasons that fell through. He also had his eyes on me, for I had made short work of one of his favorite fighters, Jack Doyle, and more recently had knocked out a new Italian heavyweight hope, Salvatore Ruggerillo. He offered to pay full transportation and living expenses in England if Max and I would come over and do battle with the empire's best. We accepted.

It was an offer that no sane men could refuse. Max took his wife, Mary, and Ancil his wife, Maudie. Two trainers, Izzy Klein and Jerry Cosale, completed our entourage. We all traveled first class aboard the S. S. Barengaria, one of the most beautiful ships in the American passenger fleet. Our five-day crossing was smooth - a surprising thing for the North Atlantic in Mid-March - and uneventful, also a surprise. Max behaved himself. I credit Mary with that.

General Critchley was no piker. Three of his aides met us at the Southampton pier when our ship docked and drove us in two elegant town cars to the hotel, which he owned, directly across the street from Buckingham Palace. For the next six months our every wish was his command. None of us had ever been treated so well for so long, either as paying or non-paying guests - and we were in the latter category.

It is possible that we might never have experienced the General's prolific hospitality if it had not been for a development in New York that helped persuade all of us to make the trip. Max suffered a suspension by the New York State Boxing Commission, on grounds that he was not physically fit to fight. The man who lobbied the commission for that completely unjustified action was none other than Commissioner Bill Brown -the very same gentleman who, for the very same reasons, tried to disqualify Max for the Carnera fight. The commission acted in the face of contrary evidence from an exam Max had taken a few days earlier, finding him to be physically and mentally fit.

Art Cohn, sports editor of the Oakland Tribune, was outraged. "As long as the public tolerates state commissions, so long will we have messes that stink to high heaven as this one," he wrote on

February 25, 1937. I agree, Bill Brown used his position of power in the boxing world to carry a personal vendetta against Max, simply because Max, by deed and word, had made him look like the fool he was. "Max will now hawk his wares in England," Cohn wrote. For that, I thank Bill Brown, because the British experience proved to be rewarding in all ways. On the other hand, maybe I shouldn't thank Bill Brown for his unintended gift, for even without his "Ban Max" crusade we probably would have accepted the General's kind offer.

Arrangements for four fights had been completed before we left the States. British promoters Sydney Hull and Bert James, at Critchley's request, worked out the details with Ancil by telephone and telegraph. Max would open on April 15 with Tommy Farr at Harringay Arena in London. I would follow on May 6 against Jimmy Wilde at the same arena. Then I would take on Jack London, reigning United Kingdom champion, at Vetch Field in Swansea, Wales, on May 24, and Max would finish the schedule against South African champion Ben Foord on May 27. It was anticipated that numerous additional matches against European, and maybe even American, fighters would follow, but that didn't happen. Too much else was going on.

Max could thank his lucky star that he was born with an ingratiating and infectious personality, for his performance against Farr left much to be desired. Farr, one of the finest and toughest fighters of our era, took Max's best punches and outboxed him for a 12 round decision. Yet Max was proclaimed a hero by the British press and public. They loved his style, his wit and humor, his "gracious manners." I was disgusted by his behavior in the ring, which in my mind was what counted. He seemed alarmed at the sight of his own blood when Tommy opened up a gash over his left eye. He dabbled at it constantly with his glove, wiped the stuff on his trunks and stared at it as if he had never been cut before. But he upset me even more with his nonchalance - as if it didn't matter that people had paid good money to see what should have been a good fight. Farr did his bit, but Max laid down on the job. But when he left the ring, thousands cheered - not because he had lost and their local hero had won, but because they liked him.

On the street, in hotel lobbies, in restaurants and pubs and theaters - wherever Max went - crowds surged around him to hear the fabled voice of the boxer who sounded like a comedian and looked like a reincarnated Greek god. He obliged everyone, sounding forth at length on any subject that came up, dropping witticisms by the dozen, all while signing autographs. He loved it all. Perhaps there is something in the British character that places more value on style and manners than in victory at any cost. Wasn't it some Englishman who said that the essence of sport is in "how the game is played?"

Jim Wilde, a Welshman from Swansea, had the same name but not the same abilities as the Jimmy Wilde of pre-World War I days, who was known as

"The Little Wonder" and who had captured crowns in Britain and Europe. But he had his namesake's courage. I'm sure that if our weights had been more equal (I outweighed him by 38 pounds) he would have given me a better account of himself, but not enough to give me a problem. As it was, I battered him to the floor three times in the first round. He was bloody and confused and on his knees when the bell saved him for continuing punishment in the next two rounds. In the fourth I slammed him to the deck twice. Each time he was up at the count of nine, but the referee, much to the disappointment of a booing crowd, stopped it. Wilde had no chance, and even though he was seemingly anxious to go on, the referee said he was in danger of serious injury and called a halt. That's what more referees should do, regardless of what the fans want or what the defeated fighter might want.

The I press was kind to me - though not overly impressed with my first effort in Britain. Geoffrey Simpson wrote for one of the morning papers that "the only things that bothered shy, good-looking Buddy, who tried to look ferocious by coming into the ring unshaven, were his long, dark hair tumbling into his eyes, and Wilde's straight left. Buddy has the same lazy stroll of his brother Max. He was rarely in a hurry about anything, and each time he hammered Wilde to the floor he assumed a quaint apologetic air. Once when Wilde slipped down, he helped him up, patted him affectionately, and considerately waited for Wilde to resume hostilities. The two days' growth of beard was a feeble disguise. Buddy is a genial young giant, who knows his own strength and feels rather sorry for his opponents."

As for my boxing abilities, Simpson had reservations. "Buddy Baer might be a world champion in the making, but at the moment this mountainous 21-years-old American is very raw...He leads clumsily, his defense is faulty, and he is slow-footed. His triumph was one of strength and size..."

Having fought a man from Swansea in London, I turned it around by going to Swansea to fight a man named London - Jack London, heavyweight champ of the isles. Good as the fight turned out to be my memories of the occasion are more of the place and its people than of the fisticuffs. If I had needed an ego trip, this one would have lasted me several years.

Wherever I walked in the streets I was surrounded by an admiring multitude. Yes, I signed hundreds of autographs, but the main thing the people wanted was to let me know how pleased they were to have me anywhere in Wales, and Swansea in particular. They shouted words of good luck in the upcoming fight, even though most of them would be pulling for their own man to win. I must have received a dozen invitations within the distance of one city block to "come on home with me, lad, for some good Welsh cooking." I didn't accept, of course, because my schedule was too tight, but I wish now that it had been possible. I've never been decisioned by a knife and fork anywhere in the world, and I would have liked to challenge the vittles served up in an average Welsh home.

The schedule called for me to visit the <u>South Wales Evening Post.</u> I was photographed sitting at a linotype machine, looking over the shoulder of a compositor, shaking hands with the editor, and balancing a secretary on one arm. Production in that newspaper came to a dead halt for the hour I was there. Writers, printers, photographers and clerks followed me from department to department. All wanted me to predict the fight, which I refused to do. When I left, police had to clear a path from the door into the street and to my waiting car. I was just a boxer, but royalty couldn't have been treated with more outgoing affection.

The fight was held at Vetch Field, a soccer stadium. I had never seen such a set-up for boxing, and haven't since. The ring was in the center, surrounded by perhaps a thousand folding chairs. In a circle around the chairs stood another four or five thousand hardy fans, sans chairs, and in the normal soccer seats, a good distance away, were the rest of the sell-out crowd of more than 13,000. The ring was covered by a canopy, and for good reason. Spring weather in Wales can change from sunshine to a rain squall in five minutes.

G. G. Lowry of the <u>Evening Post</u> had this to say about events inside the ring: "Buddy Baer proved last night that he is a credit to the ring and to the great glove game. Not once did the referee, Mr. C. B. Thomas, have occasion to lay a hand on him for holding or speak to him with regard to improper methods.

"How often, in a heavyweight contest, especially one as fierce and relentless as that of last night, does a boxer get off without once being spoken to? Frankly, I have never seen a cleaner fighter nor a greater sportsman than was Buddy Baer, and he can feel justly proud that his name will be coupled with that of his more famous brother, Max Baer, whose display of sportsmanship against Tommy Farr will be quite fresh in the memory of all.

"Strangely enough, although London did what appeared to be an impossibility; that is, staying the distance against an opponent who held all the physical advantages, it was Baer who was the better boxer of the two...I do not want to convey the impression that London was not in the picture. On the contrary, he caused Baer quite a deal of trouble ... Baer seemed to be able to take it all ... It was fairly clear that Baer could take all the punishment that London could hand out, and as each round ended with a grand slam, Baer would laugh and pat London on the back or shoulder and murmur "well done" or "good boy." Unnecessary, maybe, but they were gestures that were pleasing and sporting..."

So I won a 10-round decision, taking every round but two. Lowry ended his story this way: "I saw Buddy Baer in his dressing room afterward. He was clad only in a towel, busily signing autographs. When we had a little quiet he said, 'They don't make them any tougher or harder than London. He was great. I thoroughly enjoyed the fight, and I have enjoyed myself a lot in

Swansea. I would like to fight here again before I leave this country.'

"Mr. Izzy Klein, Baer's trainer, said he was very pleased with the fight. 'It's the first time Buddy had ever gone 10 rounds and he proved he could do it and take it. London was splendid.' Baer appeared to be practically unmarked, but London, whom I saw afterwards, was in a sorry state. Both eyes were practically closed and his head and ear were bandaged up. He had taken terrific punishment but had no complaints to make."

Max redeemed himself, in my eyes at least, in his engagement with South African champion Ben Foord. He reminded me of the Max who had toyed with Primo Carnera, striking snake-like through Foord's tough defense, retracting, pouncing again, using both hands with great effectiveness. Foord gave a splendid account of himself and would have beaten my brother if he had not been in such good form. He landed numerous sizzling punches to Max's face, but Max proved once again that he could take it and in the end knocked out Mr. Foord in the ninth round. Afterward, I got the impression he could have been elected to Parliament.

Training for our fights was a joy. We were ensconced at the Star and Garter Hotel in Surrey - another establishment owned by General Critchley. Just outside the front door a path led directly into an extensive green belt where we could run for miles without crossing a street, even though the area was in the periphery of London. Carefully tended flowers of brilliant hue flanked the pathway. The green of the countryside and wooded sections along the way made me understand for the first time the meaning of "true green." England was the greenest place I had ever seen, and I don't know how Ireland could be any greener.

For the British, our training was occasion for a daily social event. Late each morning the elegant dining room would fill up with the unlikeliest collection of boxing fans imaginable. Among the tweeds and riding britches sported by many of the men were just as many women decked out in the highest fashion of mid-day. After lunch, along about 1:30, the entire crowd would move to the hotel gymnasium where Max and I were about to commence our sparring. The price of lunch included watching us do our thing.

I use the word "sparring" very loosely. The quality of our sparring partners was so poor that we had to exercise considerable caution 'lest we hurt them. Sports writers told us that all British fighters had trouble finding competent partners for their workouts, which might explain why the nation that founded the sport of prize-fighting had been reduced to second-rate status on the international scene. I don't understand why this is so. Times were just as tough economically on both sides of the Atlantic, and such times usually produce a small army of hardened men trying to make a living in the ring. Not so in Britain -at least not then. To keep sharp, Max and I ended our sessions by knocking each other around - to the great delight of the assembled ladies and gentlemen.

It was during one of our afternoon performances - rather, afterward, when we had dressed and started mingling with the crowd -that I met a young lady of astonishing beauty who seemed to be as impressed with me as I was with her. She accepted my invitation to have a drink in one of the hotel lounges. I wanted to see more of her and asked her to dinner. She responded by inviting me to her family home. Her family home would have accommodated a dozen average families. It turned out that she was closely related to the Duke of Kent. The evening was a big success, and two days later our entire group was invited to a dinner dance at the mansion. Totally enjoyable. Elaine (I shall call her) easily found a quiet place for us to sit alone and talk. Ancil spotted us and deliberately broke up our tete-a-tete, explaining to me later that I was too young to get in over my head. I had no intention of doing that, but ridiculous as it was, he felt the need to play surrogate father and keep me from "making a fool of yourself," as he put it.

Elaine and I saw each other many times during the rest of our stay, but we were always in a crowd. General Critchley twice played host to her family, and we in turn were frequent guests at her place. Since Max and I were both involved in moviemaking, quite a few people from the studios also were on hand. We were not the only celebrities present.

It was the intrusion of the movie-makers, more than anything else, that prevented us from signing up for more fights. Max was asked by Warner Brothers to do a film called "Over She Goes," a comedy the plot of which I have forgotten. He accepted with alacrity, especially when told that his role would let him try his hand at emoting and that it would take only six weeks to make. I should remember more than I do about that film, but about the time they started working on it I was asked to work on another quickie called "Trans-Atlantic Trouble." Since I had never been before a movie camera, I worried myself silly about the project and forgot all about "Over She Goes." I needn't have worried, for I played an American boxer with championship ambitions who prepared himself for a title bout by fighting in Britain - a literal story of my real-life situation. Learning my lines was easy, for I had always been good at remembering the words for songs - dozens of songs. I coasted through my first film without forcing a single retake through a mistake of my own, while professionals around me flubbed their scenes with some regularity. I was proud of myself. Elaine said that with my voice, physique and naturalness "you ought to stay in pictures." After I saw "Trans Atlantic Trouble" I decided that I would do better in the ring.

Anyway, General Critchley had other plans for us, if we would agree. We would manage two of his hotels, one a health resort in Brighton-by-the-Sea, the other the Star and Garter in London. We could continue our fighting careers as long as one of us was always on the job at the hotels. It looked to us like a perfect set-up. The salary was excellent, our living conditions outstanding, and our opportunities for advancement bright. We accepted, and began work. Max started at

Brighton while I stayed in London, with the understanding that we would rotate on a regular basis. General Critchley was delighted with the arrangement, and as far as we were concerned we had found a new home. Then came the cable that our father was critically ill from a heart attack. We set sail for New York on the same ship that had brought us to England. Our journey to Britain ended on a sad note, but the memories remain bright and beautiful.

The trip from New York to Oakland seemed interminable. It was late September, and across the northern plains endless gray skies enveloped a landscape of corn stubble and stacked wheat, sprinkled in areas with snow - the end of life on that earth for a season. Would Dad make it through? "Oh sure," we told each other, but it wasn't until we arrived in the sun-lit Sacramento Valley that we began to believe ourselves. Survival in the warmth of California seemed a much more plausible concept than it did in the bleakness of oncoming winter on the plains of Kansas.

With our arrival at our parent's home in San Leandro - 800 Alice Street, and it's still there - it became possible to bring Dad home from the hospital. Mother alone, even with the help of Augie, Frances and Bernice when they weren't working, couldn't handle his 285-pound bulk. He had to be moved from the bed to the bathroom and back to the bed. Max and I did it easily.

Dad perked up mightily. Just having us around the house was medicine for his soul. He wasn't getting any better, but his disposition was cheerful and optimistic. We stayed until the need for money forced us back to the ring. By today's standards, medical expenses were not high in those days, but neither was there any such thing as medical and hospital insurance. We obtained professional help at home and returned to the fistic wars, Max to fight an exhibition against Nash Garrison in Oakland, and me to take on the fearsome Eddie Hogan in New York. I knocked him out in three. Before going to New York I fought a benefit match in Oakland against Chet Shandel, winning a four round decision.

Max and I both would fight once again before Dad died on May 2, 1938. I was at his side, and felt his pulse stop. Exactly three months later, on August 2, Mother joined him. They were inseparable.

TREADING WATER

Mother and Dad were buried in the Piedmont Mausoleum, where they had bought space during their Piedmont years. Max inherited their home in San Leandro. The rest of their estate - mostly personal things - was divided among Frances, Bernice, Augie and me. All of this had taken about three months a lightning swift operation by today's legal standards - but it wasn't enough time to heal our deep emotional wounds. We hadn't accepted the reality that they were gone, and talked of it incessantly.

Each of us felt the same way. Our parents had been so successful as parents that not one of us could think of any deprivation we had suffered - physically or psychologically. None of us felt that while growing up he or she had been misunderstood or in any way treated unfairly. We remembered the love, comfort, security and help we had received from them, and their love for each other, and were not ashamed of our continuing tears. We wondered if our family had been divinely touched, because so many of our friends held some kind of grudge against one or the other of their parents, or both. Whether or not that was true, we felt that we were different. Luckier, for sure.

I did have an unkind thought at the time, but the reason for it turned out to be nothing more than my own sympathy for myself. Max was getting all the attention. "Why," I thought to myself, "is so much sympathy showered on Max, and for the most part I am forgotten?" Typical of the press coverage were these lines by Art Cohn in the Oakland Tribune: "The Baers, once the happiest of households, is now one of the saddest. Max is lonesome, frightened and bewildered. There's a tragic look in his eyes."

The thought that I was the only Baer who was truly lonesome. Max had a beautiful Wife who doted on him and he was beating his chest over the birth of their first child Max, Jr. Bernice and Frances were raising families. They got support at home. I was the one who was lonely. Why didn't Mr. Cohn and his colleagues think of me? It was, of course, foolish to harbor such *thoughts, and* I soon realized that it was not so much commiseration being offered Max by the world press, but news about him. He had been the champ. He was the one who played on the world stage. He was the one who brought Mother and Dad into the limelight to share his championship year. Of course the press would focus on him in his time of personal sorrow. How dumb of me to think I should have shared equally. I was not yet a champion, and regardless of that I was being childish. A case of arrested sibling rivalry.

Mother had tried to see to it that I would never be lonely for female companionship. She wanted me to marry a lovely lass from Roseville, and had things all worked out with her family, in the Old World tradition. But I wasn't ready for such a step, and refused. Mother was disappointed, but she never criticized me for my stubbornness. "You're old enough, and God knows you're big enough, Buddy, and its time you got married," she said. "But happiness is what it's all about, and I guess you will know when the right girl comes along."

She did come along, and she was the most beautiful girl in Chicago, where we met, she at the age of 18, me 19. I was swept off my big flat feet - 20 years before Oscar Hammerstein put those words to music. I floated. I danced. I sang to the heavens. I could do anything. She was my inspiration. I told her I loved her, and she said she loved me, and I knew that Caesar and Cleopatra, Romeo and Juliet, and Douglas Fairbanks and Mary Pickford would have to make room for Buddy Baer and Shirley Solomon.

We eloped to Waukegan, a sleepy town some 30 miles from Chicago. It was so sleepy that no justice of the peace would get out of bed to marry us. Sadly, we returned to Chicago and her irate parents, who demanded to know what I had been doing with their daughter all night. Mr. Solomon soon calmed down and listened with a trace of sympathy to my story, but Mrs. Solomon was not amused. She did not want her daughter to marry a Baer. "Isn't Max your brother?" she asked. "Isn't it true that he has at least one woman in every city in America? Wasn't he running around with a crowd of show girls even while he was married?" I nodded. "Well, my guess is that you are the same type. Please go home and let my daughter alone in the future."

I was not surprised that she nixed the idea of Shirley and me getting married, but I had mixed emotions over why she slammed the door on me. I was somewhat angered by her attitude toward Max, whom she had only read about in the papers. I thought that if she knew him she would revise her opinion. But I also resented being classified as his double. Well, at least she didn't accuse me of wanting to marry into money. Mr. Solomon must have been quite wealthy. He owned several large, elegant apartment buildings in the exclusive lakeshore area of Chicago, and apparently was one of the leading real estate operators in the city. I told myself that I would not let that stand between Shirley and me. We defied Mrs. Solomon and continued to see each other, and on one occasion tried again to get married. This time we were turned down because we were under age and needed parental consent. I would have had no problem getting it, but Mrs. Solomon remained firmly negative, and I gave up.

A couple of years later she changed her mind and suggested that perhaps, after all, Shirley and I were meant for each other. By then I had come to believe that Mrs. Solomon would make herself a part of Shirley's marriage, and declined. I'm sure I was right, and no doubt Shirley eventually married the man of her and her mother's dreams. I haven't seen or heard of either one since the day I said no, but I will always remember Shirley's stunning, provocative beauty. She could have worn a gunnysack down State Street and brought traffic to an admiring halt. That I knew her was a highlight of my life.

1938 was a losing year all around. In the ring, it was the story of Gunnar Barlund, champion of Finland and one of the world's tougher heavyweight nuts. I was bigger in every way, but he had several more years of experience than I did, and he beat me in eight rounds at Madison Square Garden. Rather, I beat myself, and in so doing lost more than just a boxing contest. My pride and reputation were seriously damaged.

The date was March 4. Two weeks earlier, while in training, my sparring partner cut me over my right eye. It wouldn't heal. Ancil wanted to postpone the fight, but I foolishly insisted on keeping the engagement as arranged. I argued that I was in such good shape that I could forego sparring sessions to let the cut heal, and limit myself to roadwork and the punching bags. Ancil proved to have more sense than I did. There is no substitute for actually mixing it up in the ring to get ready for a contest that will be decided in the ring, not on the road.

I nearly won the fight in the first round. Gunnar Barlund, pride of Finland (and jealously claimed by Sweden, where he was born), looked like anything but a champion of any locale when the round-ending bell sounded. I had bounced him off the ropes on all four sides of the ring, hitting him in the mouth, forehead, eye, chest and midriff. He bled profusely. He looked too tired and beaten to continue. But continue he did, staying a safe distance through most of the next two rounds, both of which I won easily. I didn't realize it, but he had resorted to a tactic that all good boxers of the past had used as necessary, and that Gene Tunney had perfected in his fights with Dempsey. He was making me chase him, and though he sacrificed points to do it, he was setting me up for a later counter-attack.

The essence of Barlund's strategy was to tire me out, then to launch his own comeback. He timed it beautifully. In the fourth, he continued to retreat, pulling me after him, but lashed out with his left often enough to barely win the round. Three rounds for me, one for him. When the fifth began, I noticed a growing numbness in my arms. They seemed to have turned from flesh and blood to stone. For the first time, it occurred to me that I could lose unless I ended it quickly. Barlund gave me that chance. He stopped back-pedaling, went into a crouch and advanced toward me. I gave it my all, a right uppercut with all of my body in it. The blow smashed through his guard and landed square on his chin. I followed with a heavy left that caught him on the shoulder, then another right to the side of his face. He staggered into his corner where his manager, Al Remo, jumped onto the apron to give his fighter a few urgent suggestions as the referee moved in to check his condition and finally motioned him back to the ring. His head was clearing, and I had shot my wad.

In the sixth Barlund hit me with 20 straight punches to the face without a response - so I was told after the fight. I couldn't get my arms up. They were without feeling. The bell saved me from further punishment. My trainers rubbed my arms futilely during the break, and when the seventh began I was completely unable to defend myself, not to mention fight back. At the halfway point, Barlund had backed me into a corner and was pounding away at my head when the referee, Billy Cavanaugh, pushed him away and looked at my eyes. I told him I couldn't go any farther, that I had had enough. I was physically too exhausted to put up either a defense or an offense. Barlund was given a technical knockout - my first such loss. But my record of never having been knocked down remained intact.

The thunderous boos of some 8,600 fans let me know what they thought of my action in letting the fight be stopped. They paused in their vituperative whooping only long enough to cheer Barlund as he was announced the winner, then resumed delivering their message to me. As I walked shakily back to my dressing room I heard many shouts of "quitter!" and was taken aback. I was chagrined to have lost the fight, but to be called a "quitter" didn't seem right. My previous 41 fights hadn't prepared me for that.

The press, with several notable exceptions, was not kind. Most writers seemed to think that I should have fought until I was knocked out. They didn't seem to realize that by the time the fight was called I had already received enough blows to the head to have knocked out almost any other fighter. Barlund was unable to put me to sleep, but he could have done great damage to my brain if allowed to continue hitting me at will. My arms were at my side. I was a punching bag. The writers' reaction made no sense at all to me.

I blame my weakness in that fight on my lack of sparring preparation, for it was only my arms that went dead. My legs were fine, and so was my wind. Barlund, an excellent ring tactician, instinctively sensed my arm weariness and changed his battle plan to take advantage of that weakness. By staying out of my way early, he forced me into an energy sapping attack style that soon used up my strength, and he was then able to move to the attack himself, unmolested. It cost me dearly, but I learned a valuable lesson from Mr. Barlund: Don't fight unless you are physically fit; pace yourself for the possibility of having to go the distance; if you are hopelessly beaten, and still able to think, admit it and accept defeat - whatever the bloodthirsty crowd may think. It's your life, not theirs

Hype Igoe of the International News Service wrote an article for the June, 1938 Ring Magazine in which he used my Barlund fight to question the prevailing wisdom on what constitutes "courage in the ring". He said that "in England, France and many other boxing centers of the world, Buddy would not have been condemned for what the 'roar of the crowd' characterized as 'quitting.' " When a big fellow like Baer, who had punched Barlund into a giddy state... suddenly discovers that he is so exhausted that he can't get his hands up any more, is he to be derided? Isn't it a mark of intelligence to reason, while fighting that a knockout is to follow this exhaustion? Are European officials ahead of us in condoning such an action in a fighter?

"Just when should a fighter call it a day? Is a young fighter doing the right thing by himself in surrendering to defeat when weariness of arms and legs left him helpless? That was exactly the situation when Baer decided that he had had enough for that particular night. (He was wrong about my legs, they were fine, It was just my arms.) He might have taken a few more on the jaw and taken a count. He was his own jury, his own referee, his own boss. He was alone in the great wilderness they call the prize ring. Not a soul on earth could help him. He had a courageous, never-say-die veteran in front of him, and with a little over three more rounds to go, in his crumpling condition, Buddy was headed for a knockout -or complete collapse on the floor ... Buddy Baer will live down that tragedy of his young career. I'm almost certain that he will. He is a determined fellow and there is no reason why he shouldn't forget all about it and return to the ring a much better fighter."

Pat Frayne of the San Francisco Call-Bulletin wrote a long open letter to me, which included some views that nearly parallel my own on the subject: "Some day, Buddy, someone may step forward in boxing and declare that this business of knocking a man unconscious has been overdone. When this time arrives, seconds and managers will be held responsible for the condition of their fighters under fire. I have always felt that other seconds might have saved the late Frankie Campbell the night he fought your brother, Maxie. But no one stepped into the ring until Referee Toby Irwin stopped the fight without even making a count over Campbell.

"Everyone, including the referee, was blamed for the death of Campbell, but boxing itself might be blamed. It would have been cowardly for Campbell to signal that he had had enough. Better to helplessly take a beating that crushed his skull than to face the criticism of the clear-eyed, clear headed observers who were calmly viewing the procedure.

"You were helpless, Buddy, with your hands down when you signaled you had had enough. You were beaten and knew it ... You might have, in your helpless condition, taken a beating about the head from which you might not entirely recover.

"As a boxing writer I have seen many a case of a brave man of former fights who has stumbled around through life. None of your critics have much time for them, for the brave men mumble a bit and talk of forgotten glories. If someone suggests a benefit for the 'old timer,' there isn't much enthusiasm.

"There are a lot more important things to risk one's brains and life other than winning a fight. The British attitude of complacency when a fighter nods that he has had 'enough' is more in the keeping of fighting being a sport. Beating a fellow unconscious still isn't our idea of one of the finer things..."

I realize that the trouble with this kind of reasoning is that on occasion only the fighter knows the condition he is in. Frankie Campbell felt "something snap" in his head. The referee couldn't detect that, and Frankie fought on to his doom. If it had been a respectable thing for an American fighter to admit, Frankie could have saved his life by quitting at the time he suspected something might be wrong upstairs. But he would have been branded a coward, so he didn't. Few do.

Most of the time, however, the referees are in a position to see when a fighter can no longer defend himself. That is when the fight should be stopped. The sport is too dangerous to simply wait for the knockout that could turn the vanquished boxer into a vegetable - or take his life. In my fight with Barlund, the referee should have saved me the need to stop the fight myself, for I was certainly defenseless. But since he didn't, and I did, I shouldn't have been the object of the scorn that was heaped on me by most of the fight fans and the press. The verdict of the public should have been that I was soundly beaten by a strong and courageous opponent who used his superior ring experience to overcome my superior physical equipment. Period.

Of course, I know that lack of proper training caused my arms to go dead, and that my dead arms led to my defeat. I was totally confident that if in good physical condition I could defeat Barlund in a couple of rounds. I decided to go back to Oakland, spend a little time with my failing Father, then retreat to the mountains for an extended camping trip to get back in shape. As my Father got worse, and his death was soon followed by Mother's demise, I delayed the camping trip until September. I lived a woodsman's life for the next six weeks and did not fight again except for a couple of exhibitions in Honolulu - until the following March. A week after Barlund, Max more than made up for my loss. He covered himself with glory in winning a 15-round decision against Tommy Farr in New York. Farr had beaten him in their first encounter in London, and was favored by the betting boys to do so again. After all, Tommy just a few months earlier had forced Joe Louis to go the 15-round distance to win a decision and had put up a very respectable showing on offense. Mike Jacobs had promised Tommy a return match if he could get by Max. It was not to be.

The New York fight crowd welcomed Max back to their city and to Madison Square Garden with thunderous cheers as he stepped into the ring. It was his first appearance there since the Louis debacle, and it was clear from the crowd's reaction and the vast amount of press coverage he had received that he was as popular as ever before. It seemed to be generally understood that on a given day Max could beat anybody, or lose to anybody, and perhaps it was this very lack of consistency that helped his box office appeal. He was human. But whether he fought well or poorly, his great personality remained unchanged, and the public loved him for that, too.

Max was at his superlative best this night. Approaching the ring, Ancil had to keep pushing him forward as he stopped to talk with people he knew who were sitting on or near the aisle. He threw kisses to all. When he climbed into the arena and doffed his satin blue and gold robe, revealing once again the body that fight fans believed to be the most perfect ever to grace a boxing ring, pandemonium broke loose. People stood on their chairs to see him better and to applaud. Max responded with more kisses and - like a diva receiving her fifth curtain call raised both arms and turned full circle to greet his admirers.

Tommy, sitting quietly in his corner, seemed to say by his expression that he didn't mind Max getting such a reception. He would get his recognition by beating him. At the bell he came out and proceeded to fight the same way he had fought Louis - a steady advance with a two-handed body attack. Max quickly interrupted that plan with a jolting left to his chest followed by a right to the jaw. Tommy back-pedaled to gain time for his head to clear, then began his forward march again. Max nailed him with a series of rights and lefts to the body. Tommy landed a left on Max's eye, but the round went to Max.

The second round made history. Max decked him. It was the first knockdown of Farr's career - a feat that Louis couldn't accomplish - and Max did it with a left to the body. It was the first time Max had ever used his left with such authority. Tommy bounced up at the count of two and threw punches wildly, scoring twice and opening a cut on Max's cheekbone. But Max out punched him the rest of the round to give himself a two round edge.

Max also prevailed in a furious third round in which he put Farr down for a six-count, but in the fourth Farr waded into Max and actually overpowered him as they traded around 20 blows. Unfortunately for Tommy, one of his punches was low and cost him the round he had otherwise won. The fifth round was even, and Max took the sixth, seventh and eighth with a rare display of sustained boxing craft. Then, suddenly, he called a halt to what he had been doing so well and floated through the next four rounds, all of which went to Farr - mainly on the basis of his excellent jab, which was making a mess of Max's face. The crowd was restive. Was Max going to blow his big early lead? Just as suddenly as he had changed tactics in the ninth, he reverted to fierce aggression in the 13th and maintained it to the end. Farr, both eyes blackened and nearly closed, knew he had lost and left the ring as quickly as possible, immediately after the announcement. Max, who also was having trouble seeing, stayed on and on to receive congratulations and embrace his friends. He didn't need to be told that he had redeemed himself. He knew that he had put on one of his half-dozen best performances.

"I slowed down deliberately in the ninth," he told the press. "I had to pace myself, because it was beginning to look like a fight for the full distance. Tommy has one helluva jaw. I thought he would stay down in the third, but he got up and came at me like a lion. I wasn't sure I could knock him out, so I had to save my strength for the finish. It worked out just fine."

"One of the most savage fights ever staged in Madison Square Garden," wrote Henry Super for United Press. "They came to bury Max, but they stayed to praise him," said another. The writers were unanimous. Max had been intelligent, at times brilliant, proving once again that he packed awesome power in his right and could now use his left with damaging effectiveness. If he hadn't been all of that, he would not have beaten Tommy Farr, it was generally agreed. No fighter in the world, in any weight division, had earned more world respect for tenacity, endurance and raw courage than the "Gentleman from Wales."

Max at that time in his life could have signed on against virtually any fighter he chose, including Joe Louis. I don't know why he didn't. Of course, the death of our parents accounts for about six months of his inactivity, but when he decided to go back to the ring, he elected a pointless bout with Hank Hankinson in Honolulu. It was a lark for everyone. He said he needed the escape from all the sadness around home. That was understandable. He also needed the money (the bout was a guaranteed sell-out). That too was understandable. But against a fighter who had not yet won the right to fight the likes of Max?

Honolulu and Waikiki Beach, in October, 1938, came as close as any place on this planet to the visionary Garden of Eden. Downtown Honolulu was a busy port. Ships from all over the world were coming and going. Our ship, the S. S. Lurline, docked just a block away from the city's central plaza. Down the road a few miles were the Royal

Hawaiian and Moana Hotels, sitting side by side on one of the world's loveliest strands of glistening white beach, overlooked by the Diamond Head volcanic crater. The only other hotel in the area was the Halekelani, a small but elegant establishment. Don the Beachcomber had a restaurant on the lightly traveled main street. Along with a handful of other eating places, that was Waikiki Beach, circa 1938. Between there and Honolulu, nothing but open space. Looking back, I find it hard to believe, in view of what the place looks like today.

Buddy, Max and Ancil Hoffman were photographed aboard ship shortly after they arrived in Honolulu for Max's 1938 fight with Hank Hankinson.

The trip over was distinguished by more than the deep blue sea, all night dancing, and around-the-clock drinking and eating. Ancil had become irritated with Max's excesses at the table and his failure to keep up with the training schedule he had set up. Max laughed, as usual, and told "Pop" not to worry, all would be well. Angered, Ancil fired back, "Maybe I should put Buddy in there against Hankinson. You're not in shape. Buddy could whip you right now." Since I was standing right there, along with a large crowd of sunbathers on the main deck, Max felt he had to deny it. I have forgotten how it happened, but all of a sudden there was an agreement to set up a ring and let us go at it. I proved Ancil's point. We fought four rounds, and Max wasn't in it. I boxed. He swung wildly, missing most of the time. At the end he was panting, completely out of breath. Ancil pronounced me the winner of all four rounds. Max glowered, and informed the assembled throng that we were just playing around. "Nothing serious, you know." While that was true, I know that he would have liked to put me on the seat of my pants at least once.

As expected, the Hankinson fight lasted one round. Max knocked him out in two minutes and 20 seconds. I fought a couple of exhibitions, and after enjoying a few more days of Hawaiian hospitality, we packed our duds and went home. I didn't fight again until the following March. Max waited until June. We were treading water, waiting, readjusting to life without a mother or father to think about, to care for, to adore.

THE MOON AND THE MOUNTAIN

Singer Kate Smith was at the peak of her popularity in 1939, and her radio show theme song, "When the Moon Comes Over the Mountain," was one of my favorite tunes. I figured that the moon was coming over the mountain for me, that I would make big strides toward a championship match, and that maybe-other good things would happen as well. My musical taste proved an accurate forecast of the year to come.

During the Christmas season of 1938 I had been asked to sing a few songs at a "Christmas Basket" fight show put on by promoter Fred Pearl at the Sacramento Memorial Auditorium. All of the proceeds would go toward food and gift baskets for the city's needy families. I did songs between the several matches on the program, and got more applause than the boxers. Again the thought crossed my mind, "Am I a better singer than a fighter?" When the program ended I went to meet Pearl in the lobby, where I had promised to sign autographs. His daughter was with him. We were introduced. "I'm pleased to meet the mighty Mr. Baer," she said. My knees weakened and my mouth went dry. I might have thought she was putting me on, with that "mighty" stuff. Not so. I really heard only the melody of her voice, and was stricken by vocal paralysis. She flashed a dazzling smile, looked directly into my eyes, and asked, "well, aren't you pleased to meet me?" Papa Pearl slapped me on the back. "Whatta matter, son? Leave your tongue in the ring?" Finally I got it out. "Ralpha, I'm delighted to meet you. Do you sing? Your voice is music from on high - music from the spheres. Do you dance? Are you married? That's stupid of me. Of course you aren't married if your name is Pearl What's your favorite song? I like, "When the Moon Comes Over the Mountain." Do you? What..." Papa Pearl slapped me on the back again. "This is to get you to be quiet. You amaze me, son. First you can't talk at all and then you can't shut up. I'll leave you two alone for a few minutes while I check out the receipts."

I must have signed a hundred autographs while we stood there, chattering excitedly over trivia and hardly noticing the people crowded around us, pushing their programs and pads into my hands. For the first time since Shirley Solomon, I felt transported. The dingy lobby now seemed magnificent. She was better than an angel - beautiful, laughing, mocking, possessed of a voice of silver sound, and real. When we stepped to the door, now joined by her father, the corner of 16th and J Streets in one-horse Sacramento looked like Fifth Avenue in New York. You might say I had instantly fallen in love, and that I knew this was not to be a Solomon-like affair.

Ralpha was a perfect foil to my shyness. Her sparkling spirits and personality delighted me. I was surprised at my responses. Every now and then I found a witty retort to something she had said. For the first time I talked to someone outside the family about myself. I learned about her life since she graduated from high school. She continued to hold the presidency of Kappa Delta sorority and was then working as a clerk for the Department of Motor Vehicles - a state agency. After six weeks of dating for movies, dinners, picnics and trips up to the mountain snow, I popped the question in command language. "You're too talented to work for anybody as a clerk. Quit it and do what God intended you to do. Marry me and inspire me to become the next heavyweight champion!"

She seemed to know that she had drawn me into issuing that command, or one essentially like it, and grinned, impishly. "But Buddy, you are so big - and just look at me, I hardly come up to your arms. Do you really think I could measure up?" I told her that I had faith in the moon coming over the mountain to shine on us, and that my only worry was whether I could measure up. We kissed long and passionately.

Two days later we were married at a civil ceremony in Reno, witnessed by our friends Rudy Jacklich and his wife Norma. After spending a few days with her parents, and my sister Bernice, we left for a honeymoon in Hollywood, where Max was playing the good guy in a western movie, and I was to do a small role as a bad guy. To make myself look more sinister I had grown a mustache - not the bold, brave brush type that announces a manly hero, but the effete, thin, split type worn by slinking movie villains of the day. Ralpha pretended to be upset. "It doesn't work with you," she said. "You're not the slinky type. That fuzz looks like an upper lip that has just been messily involved with a hot fudge sundae. Let me pull it off!" She pulled one hair at a time, and I dutifully bellowed that she was killing me. We had a glorious honeymoon in Hollywood.

By the time I finished my few scenes in the western epic it was early February and I hadn't fought for nearly a year - not since the Barlund disaster. I felt restored, and Ralpha was providing the inspiration I needed to get back in the ring. She was more knowledgeable about the business side of boxing than I was, having been exposed to her father's work as a promoter in Sacramento. She wouldn't have had to be awfully bright on the subject to know more than I did, but it happened that she was very bright, and very interested in my future. I told Ancil that if he didn't get on the stick and arrange some moneymaking bouts I would make her my manager. He protested that it was me, not him, who was responsible for my long layoff, and advised me that Ralpha would be eaten alive by the sharpies who inhabit the business world of boxing in New York, Chicago and other big cities where the big money was to be made. I had only been joking, but I knew he was right.

Ancil wasted no time. I was signed to meet Chuck Crowell in Los Angeles on March 10. Crowell gave me a great deal of satisfaction. He was one-half inch taller, but not as heavy. Whatever the outcome, the writers would not be able to refer in their stories to Buddy Baer "towering over" his opponent.

The fight was brief. Bill Potts of the <u>Los Angeles Examiner</u> described it this way: "The fight, or massacre, lasted only 54 seconds and was over before the band had a chance to dedicate a good night number to the slumbering Crowell - 'I'm No Buddies' Sweetheart now.'

"Four times Crowell hit the deck as the cyclone of leather swished around him. The first time he took a two-count. The fourth time they could have counted two million. He was stretched out flat near the ropes with his huge toes pointing up at the ceiling and the blood bubbling from his mouth and nose.

"Crowell was so obviously badly hurt that the fans spent at least five anxious minutes waiting to see whether his handlers would be able to revive him or not. They worked on him for a full ten minutes before he could hobble from the ring. (I was shaken by what I had done to him, and called Potts to thank him for taking on the referee as he did in the following lines.)

"Crowell may have only himself to blame for his defeat, but he can thank referee Jack Kennedy for letting him get hit that one last terrific punch, which could easily have been fatal. Far too game for his own good, Crowell scrambled to his feet as quickly as his stuttering legs would let him after each of the first three knockdowns.

"Kennedy should have stopped it after the third time Crowell went down. He came up almost immediately, but he was standing there on swaying, sagging limbs with his eyes dim and glazed. He had just about managed to get his hands as high as his hips when the merciless Baer would up and let a right hand go that all but knocked the Artesia giant loose from his shoes. Kennedy finally sensed the fight was over, and instead of counting, sprang to the stricken battler's assistance."

When I threw that last punch I tried to take something off its velocity, simply because Crowell appeared to be beaten. If I hadn't been so anxious to do well, to erase Barlund from the public's image of me, I probably would have turned to the referee for instructions-before delivering the blow. I'm sorry I did it, because it was unnecessary. Yet it must be understood that most fighters lose their judgement when an opponent is in trouble and throw leather as fast as they can to finish him. The referee must be the judge, and stop the fight before serious injury or death can result.

Ralpha and I stayed in Los Angeles for me to fight Big Boy Brackey on April 4. I had knocked him out three years earlier, in Buffalo, but he had come on strong since then and was supposed to be a tough customer. He proved to be only one round better than before. In Buffalo I flattened him in one. He lasted until the second in Los Angeles.

For Max, the moon didn't get over the mountain. Joe Louis was running out of decent competition and promoter Mike Jacobs was faced with the possibility that his million-dollar baby might soon be worth a lot less - for lack of someone to fight. Max and Lou Nova were the top prospects among the serious challengers. My name was sometimes mentioned, but Ancil thought I needed another year of seasoning before taking on the Brown Bomber. So Jacobs masterminded an elimination match between Max and Lou, with the winner promised a shot at Joe.

Max had the power to drop Nova with one blow - if he could land it. He couldn't, and for ten and one-half rounds he rushed his clever antagonist around the ring, swinging and missing, taking countless jolting jabs to his eyes, mouth and nose. Nova, surely the cleverest boxer among the then-current heavyweights, toyed with him. If he had been less clever, I'm sure that Max would have knocked him out. If he had been able to punch with power, he would have knocked Max out. The referee called a halt in the 11th, when Max could no longer see through his swollen eyes.

It looked like the end of the fistic road for Max. His wife, Mary, pleaded with him to quit. So did many of his friends. I stayed out of it, thinking that he was capable of making his own decision. Finally, he said, " if that's what you want, I'll hang 'em up." He kept his word for three months.

Max had been in the limelight too long, and had enjoyed it too much, to step into the relative obscurity of retirement and stay there. Many of his sportswriter friends wondered, in dozens of columns covering pages of print, whether such a man, who still had the power to knock out any man in the world, could be serious. They recalled his glory days and speculated on what might have been - if only he had taken boxing earnestly. Max drank it all in, thirstily. Soon the publicity faded away and Max nearly died as a result. He couldn't stand the isolation not from boxing, but from the publicity that boxing brings.

He returned to the arena in September, fulfilling a promise he had made some years earlier to fight in the city of his birth, Omaha. While the citizens of Omaha made a great deal out of his return, welcoming him as if he were the reigning champion, the fight that had been arranged for him was pointless. He knocked out Ed Murphy, unknown outside of Nebraska, in the first round. Two weeks later he closed out the year by dispatching the better known Babe Ritchie in the second, in the sweltering town of Lubbock, Texas.

The weather had cooled a bit by the time I arrived in Lubbock in October to knock out Sandy McDonald in two. From there it was east to Little Rock and three rounds with Maxie Doyle, who one writer thought I carried before dropping him for the count. If I did, it was not by intention. I was just getting bored. The fight with Charles Neaves in Kansas City the next day did little to test my sharpness. He was gone in two. Then came Lee Savold in Des Moines, on Halloween night.

Savold was a hero in Iowa; his adopted state, and had won six of his previous fights by knockout. He was young and up and coming. An eastern boxing expert had named him "one of the three most promising heavyweights in the nation." Both Max and I had fought in Des Moines before, and we were popular there. Spec Taylor, dean of the city's sportswriters, was a good friend to both Max and me. I thought the city itself was exceptionally attractive. On all counts I was glad to be back.

The fight itself was nothing to write home about, but it did add a new dimension to my understanding of the fight game. I hit Savold a glancing blow to the side of his head in the first round. He fell to the canvas and a flash of pain shot upward through my arm. He rose, shakily, and I, thinking that I must have twisted my wrist out of joint, moved in to flick a few left jabs before the bell sounded. In my corner, Izzy Klein expertly massaged the wrist and probed sensitive muscles to see if I had a sprain. I didn't react, and he pronounced me fit to continue.

I finished the fight with my left hand, using the right only for feinting and as a threat. The tactic worked well enough for me to win an eight-round decision. Later that night, x-rays showed that my wrist was in good shape, but the metacarpal bone in the hand was broken. No wonder Izzy couldn't find the trouble. So now I knew what it had been like for Max to finish a long fight with one hand - and for many others in the history of boxing who have carried on despite intense pain later found to have been caused by one or more broken bones.

Beating Savold under the circumstances added more than just a victory to my record. It changed a few critical minds among the sports-writers about my ring courage.

IMPRESSING THE PRESS

From what I read in the papers, it's still true. The love-hate relationship between athletes and the press is alive and well. In 1982 there must be at least one player on every team in baseball, football and basketball who refuses to be interviewed. The writers don't understand him. He has been unjustly criticized. He has been misquoted. And so it was in my day.

Yet sport could not thrive as it does without the press, and the press would be a lot poorer if its pages were not crammed with news, opinions, analyses and predictions about sporting events. Publicity is the lifeblood of all professional athletics. Most athletes understand this, and respect it. But sometimes even the most understanding among them feel used and abused by the reporters, announcers and commentators whose words fuel the publicity machine.

My gripes are minor. Every now and then I would have liked to have punched a reporter in the nose, but far more often I felt like kissing one of the ink-stained wretches on both cheeks, buying him a drink, and thanking him for his accurate, perceptive, generous view of me. Alan Ward of the <u>Oakland Tribune</u> was one such writer. So was

Hype Igoe of the International News Service. Harry B. Smith of the San Francisco Chronicle was another. Ditto for Sec Taylor of the Des Moines Register. And there were others. These men were among my best friends, but they didn't let friendship interfere with their obligation to be honest with their readers. They, too, were professionals. When I performed below my ability, they said so. If there was a good reason for my sub-par showing, they searched it out and reported it.

And then there were those who were continuously caustic. I couldn't do anything right, even when I did well. My fight against Nathan Mann at Madison Square Garden was a good example. It took place on May 3, 1940 six months after my outing with Lee Savold. The long layoff was due to a sprained back I developed while training for an earlier fight with Mann, causing a postponement.

In the first two rounds I had things my way, belting Nathan all over the ring and holding off his rushes with my left, countering with right crosses. But I hadn't been able to throw my K.O. punch, and since the fight was scheduled for 12 rounds, Ray Arcel, my second, told me to slow up and save my strength for later.

Slowing up was not something I did well. I understood what I was supposed to do - block punches, back off, counter-punch, jab - but my execution left much to be desired. Mann nailed me on the chin with his best right in the third. I clinched and held on, though the blow hadn't hurt me seriously. In the fourth, fifth and sixth I continued to fight defensively, and poorly. Nathan captured the lead on points. Ancil had seen enough, and both he and Arcel told me to let go in the seventh. I felt a surge of relief. At the bell I almost ran across the ring to meet my tormentor. He tried to block my roundhouse right, but it crashed through to his mouth, sending him to the deck. Blood poured from his lips, but he rose at nine and I quickly nailed him with a hard left, another right, then a left, and he went down again. He pulled himself up by the ropes a split second ahead of the ten-count, and I drove a powerhouse right to his forehead. Blood oozed from the corner of one eye and the other eye was in the path of blood streaming from his brow. He wiped at it, trying to clear his eyes, then turned and walked to his corner. I leaped with joy, for he had given up and I wouldn't have to hit him again. I won the fight in one minute, 36 seconds of the seventh round.

"Sorry, but the jury on whether Buddy Baer is guilty of being a fighter is still out," wrote Lester Bromberg in The Knockout magazine. "Superficially, Buddy's seven-round knockout of Nathan Mann in Madison Square Garden constituted affirmative evidence. Still, the trend of the bout and the circumstances of the finish put justifiable doubts into the minds of the customers.

"Everybody in the pitifully sparse turnout of 5,144, which paid $11,311, agreed that Buddy was lucky to have as his opponent so 'retiring' a chap as Nate. A more valiant fighter might have carried on and outlasted the flurry in which Baer obtained his knockout...

"So when it ended there was much dissatisfaction. The crowd booed Mann, then Buddy, even as the latter waved to a friend in the ringside and yelled, 'I told you I'd get him in the seventh.'"

Critical reaction to the fight was mostly along the lines of Mr. Bromberg's prose. Even though Nathan Mann had explained that he gave up only because he could no longer see through the blood in his eyes, reporters damned him as a quitter and made light of my win over such an opponent. "Two of a kind," one suggested, referring to my "retirement" against Gunnar Barlund. If Mann hadn't stopped the fight, and I had been forced to hit him until he dropped, perhaps not to get up again, would these same critics have accused me of bloodthirstiness, maybe murder? I think so.

"We may say today without fear of successful contradiction that Mike Jacobs has no intention of carrying out his promise to toss the winner of the Buddy Baer-Natie Mann fight in with Joe Louis this summer, said Pat Robinson of the International News Service. "And for two good reasons: (1) Mike saw Mann quit to Baer in the seventh canto in the Garden last night; and (2) even if Mike wanted to feed this decidedly timid Baer to Louis, the S.P.C.A. wouldn't stand for it. This was one fight the faithful had tabbed correctly - that it was merely a question of which lad would quit first."

Mr. Robinson would have been one of the first to cry "barbarous" if Mann had been critically or fatally injured. I saw Mann's eyes. He didn't. I'm glad Mann knew enough to walk away from further damage to himself. I'm also glad that I wasn't "fed" to Louis that summer, though I thought I had done well against Mann. I wasn't yet confident enough, and my back strain continued to be bothersome. I wasn't ready for the Bomber.

Different reporters. Different eyes. Different sensitivities. Different judgements. Did Hype Igoe attend the same fight as Bromberg and Robinson?

"After a dazzling two-round start against Nathan Mann in Madison Square Garden, they said, for four rounds which followed, that Buddy Baer was the worst dub in Christendom," Igoe reported. "Then he exploded into 27 varieties of madman in the seventh, and today they talk of his meeting Joe Louis for the heavyweight title.

"Never in the history of the House that Tex Built has there been such a spectacular finish when Buddy, on orders to go out and knock him out - now is the time' - swooped down on the little fellow and crushed him into submission with all the cruel power and relentlessness of a giant war tank.

"It was an all-time surprise party for Mann, the customers, and the wise men of Broadway. They didn't know, nor did any of us, that Ancil Hoffman, Izzy Klein and Ray Arcel, in Buddy's corner, had deliberately told Buddy to 'rest up' for four rounds in order to pace himself and thus prevent a repetition of his collapse against Gunnar Barlund two years ago. Wise counsel, perhaps, yet advice which made Buddy look atrocious in the third, fourth, fifth and sixth rounds. Then came the California demon.

"As it ended, it did seem that Buddy could have done the same thing in the third had not his handlers thought best to let him pace himself. 'He'll hurt Joe Louis if they ever meet,' Mann said after the fight. 'The uppercuts will give Joe plenty of trouble and things to worry about. I was blind when the end came. I couldn't see him. It was so unexpected.'"

Igoe understood Mann's situation. He understood mine. He didn't make either of us into cowards or fools. He reported accurately. He was wrong only in his speculation that I might be ready to meet Joe Louis. As I have said, I wasn't. One month later I knocked out Valentin Campolo in the first round at Madison Square Garden. He was considered the "other giant" in heavyweight circles, matching me for height and weighing in at only 12 pounds less than my 249. An Argentine, he had beaten all of the competition in South America and had won a decision in his first North American effort, despite having been in an automobile accident a few weeks earlier that left him in sub-par physical condition. Yet Pat Robinson had this to say of the upcoming contest: "The fight mob expects Baer to have the Argentine on the deck at least six times in the first two rounds because Campolo's method of fighting is to bore in with his chin stuck out and swing punches from the heels. If Campolo can weather the first three or four rounds he may make Baer quit." Thus he managed to make Campolo look like easy pickin's, depriving me of any credit if I won, and labeling me in advance as a quitter if I lost.

In contrast, the <u>New</u> <u>York</u> <u>Enquirer</u> (no byline on the story) wrote: "The lads who frequent this fistic boulevard regard the Garden card as the best heavyweight program of the season, and they believe that out of this group of heavies will come at least one who, in the not remote future, will be sitting on top of the division. (Pat Comiskey was fighting Steve Dudas on the same program, with Pat having lost only one fight in his professional career - that to Dudas.)

"Promoter Mike Jacobs has announced that he is prepared to match Buddy Baer with Patrick Edward Comiskey, provided each comes through successfully on Thursday night. That promises to be no easy assignment for either Mr. Baer or Mr. Comiskey.

"Baer faces Valentin Campolo of Argentina, and one of the foremost heavyweights in South America, in a 12-round event. campolo hasn't shown at his best in this country as yet. But now, fully recovered from an injury that curtailed his activity, and in excellent physical condition, he is prepared to acquaint United States fans with his true merit as a fisticuffer by halting the progress of the younger Baer, who, in his last start here a few weeks ago, kayoed Nathan Mann." That advance story was fair to Campolo, and it didn't doom me win or lose - as Mr. Robinson's story did.

I never minded being rated - judged by the writers. That was, and is, an important part of the sport. I didn't mind the humor. In fact, I enjoyed it, even when I was the butt of the joke. My only complaint - and again I emphasize that it was minor - was that writers, like fighters, sometimes hit below the belt.

Max was more like the politician who doesn't care what is said about him as long as <u>something</u> is said about him, and his name is correctly spelled. Yet even he was capable of being offended. Sportswriter Alan Ward once asked him to say what he thought of the press - not the good parts, but the gripes he had about the coverage of his career. Alan quoted Max this way <u>(Oakland Tribune,</u> August 31, 1937):

"For years I've stood up against some of the shafts you boys of the press have thrown at me. I've tried to take them all with a smile ... Some of them hurt more than you imagine ... I had to take it and like it, even when I knew you were giving me a lot more rough stuff than I deserved...

"For years, while I was on my way up to the championship, and then when I held the title, I received probably more publicity than any other fighter who preceded me. You boys laid it on with black ink. You smeared me on the sports pages; you followed me up and down Broadway, both Oakland and New York. You sat by me when I ate, and you even scrubbed my back when I took a bath. When I knocked out Carnera you said I was the greatest thing in boxing shoes ... You fellows, and you fellows alone, placed me right up on the pedestal.

"First you said I was the most colorful fighter ever to hit the pike. You liked my swagger, the way I wore my clothes, the manner in which I popped off ... Then you discovered my swagger was conceit, I was a human clotheshorse, I talked too fast and loud to hide my inferiority complex, and I stepped out to some of the brighter spots because I was a burner of the midnight oil at heart.

"In truth, whatever success I had never went to my head. I never tried to high-hat anyone. The pals of my prelim days were still my pals when I was in the money ... I've been to blame for a lot of impressions spread about me, but I haven't been entirely to blame. You lads on the papers should have plenty on your journalistic conscience. Those nasty twins, rumor and gossip, have done me little good. I've been known as the 'playboy pugilist,' and I'll give you my word that I've never drunk one-tenth as much liquor as the average bank clerk, consumed as many cigarettes as most physicians, who should know better, or spent as much time in night clubs as the majority of stock and bond salesmen."

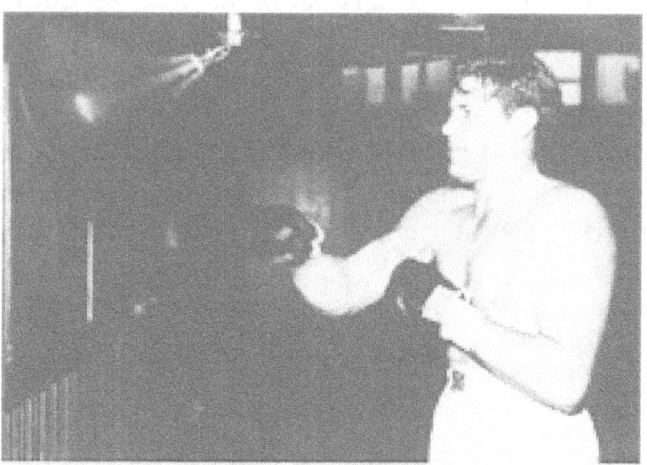

An intent Buddy Baer works on his timing as a cameraman catches the action. 1939 photo.

What Max said was literally true, but I happen to know that he wouldn't have had it any other way. At the peak of his womanizing, when he himself couldn't be sure which bedroom he would occupy when the evening sun went down, he didn't at all mind the gossip and rumor that made him into an even greater Don Juan than he fancied himself to be. Toward the end of his career, some writers called him a bum. He resented that, and felt that this low opinion of him was based more on his reputation as a night club crawler than on his performances in the ring. But he did live it up in the clubs, even though he drank very little and smoked less, so he himself was responsible for some of the worst "gossip and rumor" about him.

Max and I both benefited far more from the press than we were hurt. No one pursuing an occupation that is subject to public criticism can escape unscathed, no matter how good he may be at his work. Actors get brickbats as well as bouquets. Playwrights, novelists, historians -even reporters - take their lumps along with the accolades. So it is with boxers. I have taken a few editorial wallops below the belt. So did Max. We didn't like the low blows, but I feel that we came out clear winners from the arena of free expression inhabited by sport writers.

OUR LAST FIGHTS

On the morning of July 2, 1940, Max had three fights left in his career: Tony Galento, that evening; Pat Comiskey, on September 26; and Lou Nova, again, on the next April 4. Of course, he was not aware that this would be the extent of his fistic life. He thought that if he beat Galento he would be given another shot at Joe Louis and the title, and perhaps become the first heavyweight ever to regain the crown after losing it.

It was not to be, though Max administered a thorough shellacking to the "Walking Beer Barrel," more commonly known as "Two Ton Tony." The fight was held in Galento's hometown of Jersey City, but there was no opportunity for a hometown decision. Max knocked him out in the eighth round, eliminating that possibility.

Nine months earlier, Tony had decked Joe Louis with one of his roundhouse rights, and then failed to hold off Joe's enraged response. Even though he was knocked out, his reputation as a crushing hitter was enhanced. At the same time, Max was on the comeback trail from his defeat by Lou Nova. Mike Jacobs, sensing a major payoff if Max could succeed in his effort, arranged to match him with Tony.

The pre-battle was as colorful as the ring engagement. Tony started a war of words by calling Max an s.o.b. By way of the press, naturally. Max called Galento at his training camp to ask if he had really said that. Tony, not noted for his quick wit, said he would have to "think about it." Then, again through the press, he announced that not only was Max an s.o.b., but "so is his brother, Buddy." He boasted that after knocking Max into the fifth row, he would "chop Buddy into little pieces." Never at a loss for words, Max informed the press that Tony had better say everything he wanted to say before the fight, because he "will not be able to speak through that big mouth afterward." The press lovingly carried the messages back and forth, and a routine fight gradually was built into a big one.

Tony had enough strength to straighten the Tower of Pisa - if he could hit it on the down side with one of his haymakers. Needless to say, he could hurt you, but the probability of him landing a solid punch, .on target, was about 100 to 1 if his opponent had two good eyes with which to track its path, and two good legs with which to step aside as it hurtled harmlessly by, twisting Tony into a tortured, bulbous corkscrew.

Joe Louis must have nodded off to sleep the night he got hit by one of Tony's wild swings. Max probably was waving to a friend when Tony caught him a "terrific pivot backhand to the head" - as the Associated Press described it. Max reeled into the ropes from the power of the illegal blow, but bounced back to rain a series of his own haymakers on every section of Tony's body and head. Tony wasn't penalized for his deliberate foul - I would guess because the referee figured that any fight involving Two-Ton would be very short indeed if all of his transgressions were called. In any case, Max won the round handily.

It was a bizarre fight from the day it was announced. In addition to all the advance publicity, and the hurling of insults back and forth, Tony suffered a cut chin on the eve of the fight when his brother Russell hit him with a beer stein during a barroom brawl. From coast to coast, the engagement was labeled the "Battle of the Bums." Tony was installed as a 9-5 favorite.

Max won all but the first and third rounds, with the sixth being called even. In the seventh, Max all but put Tony to sleep, staggering him twice with explosive bombs to his tender chin. Tony would have gone down had he not, on both occasions, draped his arms around Max for support. When the bell sounded, he was virtually out on his feet. His handlers could do nothing with him between rounds, and he was unable to answer the bell, giving Max a TKO in the eighth. Again, Max was touted as a possible opponent for Joe.

Instead, the powers that be decided that Max should fight the man who was slated to be my next opponent - Pat Comiskey, a 19-year old "White Hope" who many experts thought was ready for a crack at Louis. It bothered me that I should be passed over so casually, but money will always override logic when it comes to matchmaking in boxing, and Max was thought to be a bigger draw than me. So the veteran Max and the young shooting star Pat Comiskey went at it on September 26, 1940, in Roosevelt Stadium, Jersey City, site of Max's brawl with Galento.

The two minutes and 39 seconds of action was described by the <u>Associated Press</u> as "non-stop fireworks." Pat, a 7-5 betting favorite, rushed out to meet Max and promptly tagged him with two lefts to the jaw, spun him around with a left and right to the head, then momentarily dropped his hands as if waiting for Max to fall. Max did seem to sag, but suddenly straightened up and lashed a thunderous uppercut to Pat's chin. Pat wobbled backward and fell into the ropes in a corner of the ring. Max pounced on him with another right to the head and a left to his nose, splattering blood in all directions. But Pat ducked away, danced a few moments, then drove a left hook and a right cross to Max's head. The Baer knees buckled and it looked as though he might go down. Instead, he uncoiled from an elevation about two feet above the canvas and drove his trademark haymaker upward to Comiskey's jaw. AP said "he descended like an elevator - in sections, first to the seat of his pants, then up to his knees at the count of four, then, thinking better of it, went back to the floor." Referee Jack Dempsey gave him a new count, and he rose at eight. Max smashed him into the ropes. Dempsey untangled him but didn't count. Ancil screamed his protest. Max was motioned back into action. Again he drove Pat into the ropes, where this time his head flopped onto his shoulder and Dempsey called the fight. Max by a knockout.

Strangely, rumors had traveled through fight circles before the fight that Max was to take a dive. I say "strangely" because I have no idea how such a rumor could get started. Neither Max nor I had ever been approached about a fix at any time in our careers. I think that either of us would have slugged anybody making such a proposal. The rumor about the Comiskey fight added fresh purpose to Max's performance. He was determined to ram the gossip back into the faces of those foolish enough to bet on it. In the process, he handed Comiskey a defeat from which he never recovered.

I was idle the last six months of 1940 because the fight I was supposed to have with Comiskey was awarded to Max and Ancil could not find another suitable opponent for me. I wanted Lou Nova. Ancil tried his best to get Lou Nova. But Lou wanted no part of me. It is possible for a fighter to feel in his bones that another fighter has his number. Lou had that feeling about me. With Christmas coming on, and the annual Oakland Post-Enquirer Salvation Army Christmas Basket fight show lacking a headline event, I agreed to meet Harold Blackshear, a promising young black heavyweight, on December 17 in the Oakland Auditorium.

Blackshear had not really earned a fight with me, but it was for a good cause and he had knocked out most of his opponents. Such fights are always a gamble. One lucky punch and I could lose my career. If he should lose, it would be considered part of his learning process, because of my greater experience and high ranking. I took few chances in that encounter, boxing him cautiously in the first, opening up in the second, and knocking him out in the third. For me, the most exciting part of the evening was the presence of Jim Jeffries and Tom Sharkey and a host of other boxing greats from years gone by. Jim refereed one of the preliminary bouts, and Tom - who had lost to Jim in two titanic struggles - appeared with Jim in a center-ring ceremony. I was awed when they came to my dressing room after the fight to wish me well. What do you say to legends? Max would have no trouble, but I was tongue-tied.

Max was now the people's choice as No. I challenger to Joe Louis. I was rated by some as No. 2, by others as No. 3 after Lou Nova. Within four months, both of us fell from these lofty rankings. I was the first to stumble.

Eddie Blunt, a powerful black from Harlem, had stopped Abe Simon in 1940 - the only one to do so - and had also beaten Tony Musto, who in a few months would force Joe Louis to go nine rounds. Earlier, he had lost decisions to Tony Galento and Red Burman, but was considered a worthy opponent for me in January 1941, when the pickings were none too good. It was another gamble, and I lost.

Early in the fight Eddie poked me in the eye with the thumb of his glove. This is a tactic that many fighters use. It's called the "gouge," and it can blind the victim for hours in the affected eye. Just recently, in the spring of 1982, it was proposed in California that boxing gloves be made without thumbs. I think it would help. Maybe the gouge as we have known it all these years would be eliminated. But the laces would remain, and they can be used to perform a similar operation on the eyes.

I fought Eddie with one eye from about the third round until the finish. He cut me on the cheek in the fifth, which made for a lot of blood but it didn't hurt my performance. I just couldn't see well enough to land a really solid punch. We mainly boxed for ten rounds. Most writers scored it a draw, but the officials - who also had called it even for nine rounds - awarded the decision to Eddie on the basis of his greater aggressiveness in the last round.

To be beaten by anyone is always hard to take. To be beaten by an unranked fighter is a disaster. For a few dark days I toyed with the idea of quitting the sport. When I expressed the thought out loud, Ralpha, a true daughter of a fight promoter, sensed that I was looking for a little domestic encouragement and kissed me on my still-bandaged eye. "Stop it," she said. "You are in the best condition of your life, and you haven't yet fought Joe Louis. You know that you won't quit until you do, so please stop the retirement talk. Besides, I want you to go on."

In April, Max fought Nova the second time. Somehow, the impresarios of the sport concluded that despite Max's popularity with the fans, he should not be matched with Louis until he had defeated the only other man who had beaten him without a return beating. But Max had the same kind of feeling about Nova that Nova had about me. Nova had his number.

The fight was a replay of their first meeting, except that this time Lou battered him senseless in eight rounds instead of the eleven he needed earlier. It should not have been. I respect the ability Nova brought to the ring, but Max was a far better fighter in every department but one. Nova was a better boxer. Max, by scorning the art of ring craft throughout his career, created his own Achilles Heel. Every fight he lost - including, possibly, the Louis defeat - could have been reversed if he had been able to box with average skill. He relied entirely on his powerful right hand, augmented in mid-career by a dangerous left, and his capacity to absorb punishment while waiting for an opening. But there was a limit to how much he could take while retaining enough strength to retaliate, as Nova proved. Earlier in his career, I am certain that his power would have overcome Nova's classic style, as he demonstrated in his second fight with Ernie Schaaf. In fact, he almost put Nova away in the fourth and fifth rounds of their rematch, but didn't follow through.

If ... If...If Max had only learned to box. He would have handled Nova the first time, and probably would have had a second chance with Louis. As a boxer and slugger, he might have become the first heavyweight to have regained the championship. As it was, he retired, personally humiliated, but still - in the eyes of millions of fight fans the world over - the most exciting fighter in history and the most spectacular example of unrealized fighting potential the ring had yet seen.

Four days after the curtain dropped on the career of Maximilian Adelbert Baer, I stepped into the Uline Ice Arena in Washington, D.C. to face Tony Galento. On the same night, in St. Louis, Joe Louis was to make his 16th title defense against Tony Musto. Joe was an overwhelming favorite to win. I was a 7-5 underdog. But if I should win convincingly, I would move ahead of Billy Conn and Lou Nova in the ongoing contest to find opponents for Louis. (I should mention at this point that a match between Billy Conn and me was never considered because of the weight differential - he being at the top of the light heavyweight division, while I was a heavy heavyweight.)

On the night of April 8, 1941, however, I was not the heaviest of the heavyweights. Tony Galento checked in at 247. I was down to 240. But it was no contest. I hammered Tony almost at will for six rounds. He was a bloody mess. I was unscathed. At the bell he lurched into his corner and yelled that his hand was broken. Jimmy Frain, his handler, promptly cut off the glove on his right hand while the referee stood by objecting loudly. When the bell for Round Seven sounded I came out to fight, but Tony was still sitting on his stool, minus a glove. I was given a TKO in seven. Tony's purse of some $5,000 was held up by the boxing commission until the condition of his hand could be ascertained. X-rays showed a bad bruise, but no break, and 24 hours later he received his purse. His handler was suspended for 60 days for cutting off his glove without the referee's permission.

The press was less than ecstatic about the caliber of my victory, leading me to again wonder what the hell it was I was expected to do. Kill my opponent? One-round knockouts didn't satisfy my critics. A knockout in any round failed to please. A win by decision was tantamount to defeat. In the case of Galento, was I expected to put him to sleep? Not even Louis had done that. Whatever the critics said, however, meant little to the promoters, who were guided exclusively by the profit motive. At this time it was decided that I would make the cash registers ring faster and louder than either Conn or Nova, so I was selected to face the fearsome Louis the following month at Griffith Stadium in Washington, D.C.

There was enough controversy about my defeat by Louis, which I have already described, that a second match was considered necessary. I waited patiently for the rest of the year to get a second chance, but it didn't come until after the Japanese bombed Pearl Harbor on December 7. With the war on, and the nation swept by patriotic fervor, Mike Jacobs did his bit for his country by arranging for Joe and me to meet on January 9, 1942 at Madison Square Garden, with the proceeds earmarked for the Navy Relief Fund. It didn't cost Mike a dime, of course, and I wouldn't be surprised if he managed to pocket some of the $65,000 gate. Joe and I received nothing other than compensation for training expenses already incurred.

During the short training period, I was unfortunate enough to be riding in a car that was hit from behind by another motorist. The collision snapped my head backward so violently that I still suffer the consequences. Ancil requested a postponement, but Jacobs fairly screamed that this fight was for Navy Relief and it was our patriotic duty to be good soldiers and carry on. We agreed - stupidly, for a postponement would have made for a much better fight than the one-round fiasco that resulted. Joe's first punch was to the side of my head. The pain - the most intense I had ever felt - immobilized me. I couldn't turn my head without turning my body. I tried to fend off Joe's next rush, in vain. He hit me as he pleased. I went down - not out, but for the 10-count. The fight, and as it turned out, my career in the prize ring, had ended. A short time later, Max and I together joined the Army Air Corps.

BEDTIME FOR BUDDY

I regret to say that I have no war stories to tell my three grandchildren or anyone else. I never fired a gun except in training. I didn't serve overseas. I wear no medals for distinguished service. The only physical scars I carry from my years as a soldier are from bedsores picked up from a score of military hospitals in every corner of the U.S.A. I have nothing to brag about, and nothing for which I feel the need to apologize, though I do regret the way I was compelled to fight the war.

Max and I were inducted together on December 15, 1942, at McClellan Army Air Force Base in Sacramento. The event was given saturation coverage by the press, partly because of pressure from the Army public relations people. One of the publicity stunts involved three WACs (so-called for Women's Auxiliary Corps) sitting on my shoulders and outstretched arms, smiling and posing for the photographers. When I tried to gently put them back on the ground, I pulled a ligament in my right leg. So instead of going with Max to basic training at Fort Ord in Monterey, I was shuffled off to Letterman Army Hospital in San Francisco, where "Brick" Muller, the famous University of California football star, by then a surgeon specializing in leg injuries to athletes, performed the operation. For years, Muller had been one of my heroes. I had read many times of his exploits for the Golden Bears of Berkeley, the most spectacular of which was a pass that went 80 yards in the air for a touchdown in the 1921 Rose Bowl game against Ohio State. He, on the other hand, thought I had all the stuff of which heavyweight champions are made, and treated me as it I had actually been one. For us, it was mutual admiration week.

Max and I were outsize for the Army Air Force, which was embarrassed to find following our induction, that no uniform in stock was big enough to fit us. We would have to wait several days for special uniforms to be made. An alert noncom, who earned a few extra bucks by selling "custom mades" to men unhappy with their ill-fitting garb, offered to equip us with perfect threads within 24 hours, for $50 each. Max agreed, for he wanted to show off his military splendor on his weekend leave. I decided to wait for my official duds. My uniform arrived before his, so he was out $50 and I was one-up on him in the first week of our new competition - military style.

My leg healed perfectly and quickly. After a speed-up course in basic training at McClellan, I joined Max in a special assignment visiting bond rallies and representing the air force at sporting events and other large-scale happenings where we could appeal to the public to buy bonds. After about six months of this pleasant duty we were reassigned to Wright Patterson Field in Dayton, Ohio, and before we could unpack were ordered to report to the Pentagon. On the train to Washington, D.C. we speculated that we might be sent to England because of our fighting experiences there and our knowledge of the people. But no, we were to become morale builders at air force command bases scattered throughout this country. Our schedule would have frightened even a veteran vaudevillian.

With a lieutenant and a staff sergeant assigned to lead the way and make advance arrangements, and with orders to "keep to your schedule by using any means of transportation possible," we became accustomed to 4 a.m. departures and 2 a.m. arrivals, with performances running from 8 a.m. to late at night. We boxed each other to illustrate fine points of the sport to boxing teams on each base. We held boxing classes. We visited patients in local hospitals. We taught physical fitness, ran programs in calisthenics, demonstrated uses of bodybuilding tools, and gave short speeches on the vital necessity of strong bodies in the combat that was to come.

We traveled by military and commercial aircraft, trains, busses, and military and private cars or trucks. We traveled to bases in Utah, Texas, Oklahoma, Florida, Ohio, New York, North Carolina, Arkansas, Nebraska, South Dakota, and Tennessee, where I met my personal Waterloo. Early in our tour, it was decided that Max and I should no longer box each other in demonstration matches. We were getting too rough. Instead, we would box volunteers from each base. By and large, this proved to be a much easier routine.

Some mighty big and tough men stepped through the ropes, hoping to knock one of us on our butt and live to tell about it, but of the hundreds we met only one gave Max any trouble at all - I flattened him, much to Max's chagrin - and one at a Tennessee base gave me 'a pain in the neck. He was small and wiry. To hit me on the head he had to leap and swing while airborne. One such swing landed on my neck, which had never fully healed from the auto accident just prior to my second fight with Joe Louis. Later that night, I realized from the growing pain that the injury had been seriously aggravated. When I asked to be taken off the tour, the Pentagon sent me to a hospital in Florida. It was the beginning of a long, close, and sometimes controversial relationship with military medicine.

By this time it was January 1944. The doctors in Florida, one of whom was a specialist flown in just to check on me, decided that traction would be required for the next three months. I came to know how much one can learn about a ceiling by staring at it. My vision seemed to improve to the point that I could count the flyspecks, separate the paint into molecules and determine the shape of each. I wrote songs in my head poetry too, limericks mainly. And I acquired bedsores numbers one through eight.

Before I was let out of traction, I found that Max had been admitted for similar treatment, and accused him of gross imitation. I said, "Who's the big brother now? It's me, isn't it? Everything I do, you do." He was not amused, because, in fact, he really had hurt his neck - though it was through his own reckless behavior, showing off to the troops by throwing sandbags in the air and catching them on the back of his neck.

A few days before Max became a patient I was startled to see one of the world's most famous and admired women come through the door, flanked by two nurses, and head straight for my bed. I had never thought of her as beautiful, but after about five minutes of trying to answer her questions about my progress, and what I planned to do after the war - and after hearing her speak of other patients she had seen, and pass along some good news about how the war was going in Europe and the Pacific, I thought she was as beautiful as my mother. Eleanor Roosevelt glowed with compassion, yet she was unmistakably strong in her conviction that we were fighting a just war and that the post-war world would be a better world. Marie Dressler was not a beauty queen either - I knew her well -but she was beautiful in my mind. Just like Eleanor. Yes, Max was upset that he hadn't been honored by a visit from the First Lady, but he wasn't there. The way we counted such things in the military, I was now three up.

My *condition did* not improve. Three hospitals and five months later I was returned to McClellan Field to make a tour of European bases with Red Ruffing, a pitcher for the New York Yankees, and John Samayel, the national ping-pong champion. The war was over, over there, but troops would be needed in large numbers to keep the peace until *international agreements* had been worked out.

Before we could leave, Congress approved the immediate release of anyone over age 44. Ruffing qualified, and asked for his discharge. Then it came to the attention of my *commanding officer* that I was physically unqualified for overseas duty. He threw our travel documents in the air and roared, "Why does not someone tell me what's going on!" Instead of Europe, I was sent to Camp Lee in Virginia for a physical profile.

My Colonel who first saw me at Camp Lee had his own ideas about my future. After glancing quickly through my records he accused me of "trying to make money in the army by using your Jewish religion - you and Max both. You're no more Jewish than the man in the moon." I was stunned. I had never used my Jewishness for any purpose in the army, least of all to make money. I was about to respond when he ordered me back to basic training. "What about my physical profile?" I asked. "You've had enough medical care," he snapped.

I went straight to the Inspector General's office. He invited me in for a smoke and asked me to tell him "everything." I did, with emphasis on the fact that one hospital after another except for the first one in Florida - practiced confinement without treatment and showed little interest in getting at the cause of my condition. I was still physically unfit for normal duty assignments. He sent for my records, then informed me that I had a "legitimate bitch." Within days, I was given a discharge on medical grounds.

No war stories.

CAMERA, LIGHTS, ACTION

By today's standards, Max and I were paupers when we put away our gloves and contemplated retirement from the only occupation we had ever known. At the end of the war Max was only 36 and I was still in my 31st year - ages when most young men are just getting started in their careers. But, as boxers, we were burned out - Max because his lifestyle had taken its toll, and also because his age was the normal outer limit for boxers who valued unscrambled brains- me because of my neck and assorted other injuries. And then there was the fact that we had been inactive for nearly three years of military service. The combination compelled us to look elsewhere for means to make a living. In his career Max threw away a substantial fortune, as fortunes were measured in the 'thirties and 'forties. I never earned a fortune to throw away. My biggest payday was not as a challenger for the crown, or as the main attraction in other major fights, but as a preliminary fighter. I earned $41,000 in my bout with Ford Smith, which was a preliminary to Max's fight with Joe Louis. By comparison, I made only $ 29,000 in my two fights with Louis. A more typical payday was around $5,000. Take home pay was a good deal less, for travel and training expenses had to be deducted, and taxes also took a bite. Several of my fights actually lost money or barely broke even.

Max was saved financially by the man who did more than anyone else to damage his fistic reputation. He had not saved a dime up to the time he fought Louis. Dad was angry with Ancil Hoffman for not exercising some control over Max's spending habits. Ancil pleaded that it would be easier to control the weather than to influence Max's way with his wallet, but promised to try. I really don't know how he managed it, but he persuaded Max to let him invest his entire purse for the Louis fight in an annuity that would pay him a monthly stipend for life. So, as Max faced the post-war world, he could look forward to a minimum income that would maintain his family in comfortable style.

I wasn't quite as lucky, but I was not without some resources. Back in 1941 I had bought an interest in a Sacramento bar, just across the street from the state capitol building. My partners were Don Ricci, and Jackie King, a Sacramento fight promoter. Naturally, the place was called "Buddy Baer's," to take advantage of the business my name would bring in. We did very well. Many legislators and state employees were regular customers, along with a growing number of military people from nearby air bases that were expanding as the war in Europe became more and more critical. A big attraction was the piano player, a beautiful young thing by the name of Helen Tweedy. She could play just about any song that was requested, and accompanies any set of vocal cords in any key, no matter how off-key most of the singers were.

We had a standard procedure with the music, at my insistence, if too much time went by without anyone asking me to sing, I would whisper to a trusted ally to start a chant, "We want Buddy! We want Buddy." Then I, with a feigned show of exasperation, would accede to my public. "Well, if you're all tone deaf, or pleasantly plastered, or both, maybe you can stand listening to," I would say, and then give them the name of the first of several ditties I would sing. They thought I was a combination of Caruso and Sinatra. And like all hams, I ate it up. I really enjoyed that bar.

I took care of the soldiers and sailors as if they were members of my family. If they had too much to drink and passed out, I made them comfortable in an out-of-the-way part of the bar. If they missed their last transportation back to their quarters, I took them there myself after the bar closed. If they looked as though they were about to have one too many, I would advise them to wait awhile - and I can't think of a single instance when they gave me any back talk. If they began to throw their money around foolishly, wanting to buy drinks for anybody who walked in, I cooled them off. My bartenders were trained to remember that these were kids, most of them away from home for the first time, and most of them making their first acquaintance with demon rum. For them, our bar was just as homey and a lot more protective than the local pool hall back in Junction City.

During the war, a group of soldiers stationed on a stretch of sand called a South Pacific Island built a small shack and placed a sign as big as the shack on its roof. "Buddy Baer's II," it said. I know, because they sent a picture of it to Buddy Baer's I, and I saw it while I was on home leave. We placed it, reverently, on the back bar, where it stayed until I sold my interest in the place in 1948.

Today, when I walk by the real estate office that occupies the sacred space once known as "Buddy Baer's," I find myself blinking a little faster. The bar was more than just another drinking establishment. It was a rendezvous for lovers, a little theater for aspiring magicians and vocalists, a stage for banjo players and guys with guitars and horns, a post office address for out-of-towners, place for political intrigue (our four walls, along with those in three other nearby bistros - Frank Fats, Bedell's, and the Senator Hotel - were silent witness to as many political deals as were being recorded in legislative chambers across the street). And it was Radio City Music Hall for me. I loved the place.

I wouldn't have sold my interest if it hadn't been for Bud Abbott and Lou Costello, who were in town to do a show at the State Fair. I had met them earlier in Hollywood, but Lou was a close friend of Don Ricci's and they were schoolmates back in New Jersey - so they dropped in the bar primarily to see Don. "When are you going to do another picture?" Don asked. "Just as soon as we find a couple of heavies to be our villains," Lou answered. When they said they needed two big men who could act well enough to get by but not well enough to steal the picture, Don suggested, "what about Buddy and Max?" Mr. Abbott and Mr. Costello promptly fell off their stools, kissed Don on top of his head, and yelled, "perfect!"

At that moment I was across the room, listening to some customers at a table exchange the latest jokes. Abbott wandered over, climbed on a chair next to where I was standing, and put his arm around my shoulder. "Have you ever heard this one?" he asked the customers. "Who did Mother Nature intend to be the biggest actor in Hollywood? If you don't say 'Buddy Baer' I won't buy a drink." They all sang out, "Buddy Baer, now buy us a drink." Abbott bowed, and motioned to the bartender to bring over a round. He stepped down from the chair, moved it directly in front of me, climbed up again and put his face about six inches from my nose. "Africa is screaming for you," he announced. "Africa Screams cannot be made without you - you and Max. It will be our greatest hit. How about it?"

When he explained that "Africa Screams" was the name of the new movie he and Costello were about to make, and that neither Max nor I would have many lines to learn, I accepted for myself and promised to persuade Max to add his magnificence to the cast.

All I needed to do was ask. Max was suffering from the painful disease that afflicts all natural-born hams when they are no longer in the spotlight. Sure, Max was a big hero around Sacramento, and still drew admiring stares and whispers of "that's Max Baer" wherever he went, but that wasn't enough. Not after you've been a world celebrity. "Of course I'll take the part," he said with a big grin. "Naturally, I expect to get the girl. Tell Abbott and Costello to get those cameras ready to roll. Maxie is coming to town."

Max had been to that town - Hollywood - many times before; most recently in 1946 when he and ex-light heavyweight champion Maxey Rosenbloom teamed up in a highly successful comedy revue at Garay's Copacabana. They sang and danced and joked and clowned and between them made $3,500 a week doing what came naturally. Rosenbloom matched Brother Max hambone for hambone. Their most popular number in the revue was called, "All of a Sudden My Head Rings."

Max was not going to get the girl in "Africa Screams," but he had enough talent to be the leading man in any movie ever made by those lovable loonies, Bud Abbott and Lou Costello. Back in 1940 he played the lead in a New York musical called "Hiya Gentlemen," with Sid Silvers. The farce concerned a con man, Spinner Skinner (Max) who faked his credentials to gain admission to Groton State College, where he set up a bookmaking operation in the dormitory. Silvers, a comic genius, played his bodyguard. Between them they involved the entire student body and half the faculty in their antic operation. Max had to learn 150 pages of script, and did it easily.

My stage experience had been limited to a brief appearance with Max in a western, plus the movie I made in England, and Buddy Baer's bar. For "Africa Screams," experience was unnecessary.

I spoke two words, but loomed large on the screen for most of its length. Max spoke five words, and also loomed large. Neither of us was nominated for an Oscar, but the movie made a lot of money.

When the movie was completed, Max stayed in Hollywood long enough to help out with some advance publicity and make a couple of radio commercials, then returned to his loving family in Sacramento. His marriage was a complete success. He and Mary had three children - Max, Jr., Maudie Marian and James Manny - all of whom he adored. They were looking forward to building a new home on five acres of land in the Sierra foothills that had been given to him before the war by Larry Cameron, a wealthy automobile dealer. (As it turned out, they never built their dream house, but their land is now part of a huge, beautiful residential development known as Cameron Park.)

Max did a lot of public relations work for Cameron before and after the war. He considered this work his main occupation, but he also was in demand as a referee for boxing and wrestling matches. His presence in the ring added thousands of dollars to the box office receipts. In fact, he and I both were offered fat contracts to become wrestlers, but we declined. I couldn't have accepted because of my neck injury, though I would have refused anyway because, much as I liked show business, professional wrestling seemed to have too complicated a script. I would never have learned how to take a dive, or how to beat my chest in triumph and act like a victor when my opponent took his dive.

I stayed in Hollywood - a bachelor on the loose in the midst of the world's greatest concentration of feminine pulchritude. Ralpha and I had drifted apart during the war, and even though we were blessed with my only child, Sheila, we were divorced in mid-1943. There was no "other woman" at the time, but shortly afterward, while I was an outpatient at the hospital in Florida, I did meet a highly attractive, personable lady by the name of Ruth Boyington. She was the daughter of a friend who operated a nightclub in Palm Beach. From the time we were introduced we knew we had a future together. It began with a series of dates whenever I was on leave from the hospital. Finally I was released from the hospital and returned to McClellan Field in Sacramento. Ruth came with me. A few weeks later, in March 1944, we were married.

This marriage lasted until October 1947 when it ended in divorce. Again, as had been true with Ralpha, it just sort of died on the vine. There was no animosity between us. We liked each other very much, but the spark that makes a marriage work was gone. Today, 35 years later, we are still good friends. She is married to Tommy La Presti, a Sacramento golf pro who also is a good friend. My current and permanent wife, Vicki, and I visit with them often. The same pleasant situation prevails with Ralpha, who is married to Dr. Roger Daniels of Sacramento. He is my doctor. The four of us see each other socially on many occasions. Vicki calls me "Jacob, the Peacemaker."

But, in 1949, I was unencumbered. And, like a wolf in a meatpacking house, I didn't know when to stop admiring my surroundings and reach out for one of the many beauteous damsels who seemed to be at my beck and call. I learned, however, and within three months lost 30 pounds - down to my fighting weight. Life was good.

Abbott and Costello had signed me to do a new picture, "Jack and the Beanstalk." For the first time in my life I had a voice teacher Herbert Wall, the very same man who taught Nelson Eddy. I also had an agent, and the agent was busy lining up singing engagements for me. I sang at some of the most famous clubs in the country Leon and Eddie's in New York, the Mocambo in Los Angeles, among others and I couldn't believe the reviews.

"Buddy Baer carousing before a chichi New York mob at the Plaza Persian Room is a mighty singer," said Earl Wilson. "Buddy Baer is the greatest singer I've ever heard," wrote George S. Kaufman. "A solid new act here to stay and shine," Variety proclaimed. "As a singer Buddy Baer is a knockout," said Danton Walker in the New York Daily News. "Buddy Baer has the greatest natural voice in America today," said Herbert Wall, without an apology to Nelson Eddy or any of the truly great singers in the nation. I was flattered by the hubbub, but I really didn't believe my press clippings. There was no way I could be that good, I said to myself. Perhaps, if I had believed in myself more than I did, I might have remained a professional singer for the rest of my working life. As it was, I reacted to my instant success on stage as I did to my early successes in the ring - with a touch of fright over what was expected of me, followed by a subconscious retreat, so slight that I didn't recognize what I was doing. Can you imagine me as an operatic tenor? Serious people said I could be if I wanted to be. I made the easy choice. I disbelieved.

Buddy and his second wife Ruth Boyington, at the time of their marriage in March, 1944. Buddy met her while he was on convalescent leave from a Florida military hospital.

But I kept right on singing the songs of Tin Pan Alley and the musical stage, first because I loved them and so did the public, and second because they offered little in the way of a challenge to the development of my vocal potential. Also, I was having a grand time. At least as good as Caruso or Melchior or Tibbet did. I sang not just for the paychecks, but for the sheer joy of it. When I was a visitor in various night clubs, people would call out for me to do my thing, and I did so happily - just as when I vocalized for the people in my own bar.

Naturally, I played the giant in "Jack and the Beanstalk" -another solid moneymaker for Abbott and Costello. This time, however, I had more lines to speak and a character to develop. Louis B. Mayer noticed that I was not just an ex-pug playing an ex-pug, but an actor of modest ability. He asked me to become a member of the MGM family, but my agent advised me to remain a free agent and sign with MGM on a picture-by-picture basis. In the next several years my name appeared high on the marquees of the nations theaters as movie after movie rolled out of Hollywood's fantasy factories with me playing more and more significant roles. I was making it in Hollywood without "going Hollywood."

"Going Hollywood" in my mind meant letting any measure of success, large or small, go to your head and lead to fat-headed behavior. It meant fawning on people who were more famous than you, or in a position to help you, and ignoring the others. It meant pretension and fakery. It meant living without personal commitment to anything or anyone other than one's self. It meant having opinions of infinite flexibility, instantly adaptable to those of whomever you wished to impress. The really big stars in Hollywood knew all about that, and insisted on being true to themselves. Newcomers, like me, were all too susceptible to the malady. But I had too much of Livermore and South Oakland and Sacramento in my blood to be infected. That is probably why my third marriage was another failure.

I met May Mann at a party in the Mocambo for a dozen or so stars, of the stage and screen and the athletic world. Rita Hayworth and Ali Khan,

Ilona Massey, Joan Crawford, Sonny Tufts, Lou Nova, Tommy Harmon and Jack Dempsey were among those present. I wandered over to a table where there was an empty chair and asked if I could sit down. "I'm May Mann," said the lovely lass in the other chair. "That seat is for my date, Jack Dempsey. He's coming later. But you can borrow it until he shows up. Can you defend yourself?" I proudly said that Jack and I were old friends, and that I wouldn't think of hitting him. She was amused. "Can I quote you on that?" she asked. "In case you don't know, I write a daily column and contribute articles to about ten magazines in this town, so watch what you say if you don't want your name in print. But who in this room doesn't want his name in print?" It was my turn to be amused, but I was fascinated as well by this extremely pretty, teasing, worldly woman.

"How about dinner tomorrow night?" I asked. "And the fights the next night?" I really didn't expect her to say "yes," but she did -possibly because another woman, Denise Darcel - Tarzan's newest film playmate - was making what she interpreted as "brazen passes" at me. I'm usually very much aware of such delightful happenings, but I must have been paying too much attention to May Mann to notice. I suspect, however, that it was Miss Darcel more than me who was responsible for May's interest in me.

Surprisingly, May seemed to enjoy the fights. She even claimed to enjoy my newest picture, "Giant from the Unknown," in which I played my first lead role. The critics disagreed with-her.

Ballgames, the racetrack, the Planetarium, the beach - whatever we did, she enjoyed. If we had done nothing more than sit and talk, I would have enjoyed just being with her. But she had enough sex appeal to generously endow six women, so that was not all we did. Of course, we got married.

If publicity is the mother's milk of entertainers, I was the healthiest kid on our block. May had to be a little bit careful of how often she lauded me in her various stories - after all, she was a newswoman and as such was supposed to be objective - but even so I fared well. Not only did she write of things I had done, she glowed with confidence over the things I was destined to do. She made much of the fact that a group of girls - all carhops at a local drive-in restaurant - had given me their annual "Heartthrob Award" - in this case, an oversize, idealized portrait of myself, inscribed, "The Working Girl's Clark Gable - So Much More of You to Love." (She treated it as a joke, which it may have been. I was vain enough to think it might be a sincere expression by star-struck youngsters, and went to the drive-in to thank them. I'm glad I did, for it pleased them mightily.) I don't know whether or not May's publicity helped me land new roles, but I'm sure it didn't hurt.

For the first two or three years my movie career was a succession of roles that took advantage of my size. In addition to "Jack and the Beanstalk," where I was, of course, the giant, and "Giant from the Unknown," there was "The Magic Fountain" and "Quo Vadis" - the most expensive picture ever filmed up to that time, set in ancient Rome and starring Robert Taylor and Deborah Kerr. I played Ursus, a giant bodyguard.

Ursus was charged with protecting the lives and safety of several important people in Nero's government, including Deborah Kerr. He had three big fight scenes, but in order for them to work as the script intended he had to be seen as far more than a powerful, skillful athlete. It was my job to bring out his intelligence, warmth, loyalty and understanding of political power and intrigue. I had to act at a higher level than ever before.

The first of the three fights was easily staged, with me beating the champion gladiator of the great Roman Empire. The second was harder to make realistic - I had to defeat seven powerful litter carriers (men who carried imperial personages and their trappings of state on bejeweled, brocaded platforms), not one at a time but as a group. The third, climatic scene was my struggle with a 2,000-pound Italian bull with a six-foot horn spread. Actually, I could have thrown the bull in a lot less time than the script required. It was very difficult to carry El Toro through sequence after sequence where I narrowly missed being gored, for the purpose of building sympathy for me rather than him. I had to be thrown to the ground several times and evade the very real rushes of the bull before, finally, I was allowed to seize him by the horns and twist his massive neck until he flopped on his side.

I survived all of this without any physical damage other than a swollen knee caused by a nip from the bull's horn. But I still carry a scar from a lion that was not in any of my scenes. I passed too close to his cage on the set and he flashed a mighty paw between the bars removing half a pound of flesh from my right shoulder. MGM said they would be glad to return the missing tissue in artificial form, but I declined. Since I had no war wounds of which to boast, I now had something just as impressive to show my grandchildren - a permanent memento from the king of beasts.

The picture, made in Rome, required nearly a full year of shooting. I was there, accompanied by May, for 24 weeks from May to November at $1,000 a week. Robert Taylor made that much in an hour or so, but when the movie was released it was little old me who got the rave reviews. "The big surprise in this epic film is Buddy Baer, who proved what many have suspected for some time. He is a natural actor. His portrayal of Ursus is perfect. He comes close to stealing the picture." So said one critic in words that reflected the general consensus. I was quickly signed for more big-budget blockbusters.

In "Jubilee Trail," with Forrest Tucker, John Russell and Joan Leslie, I sang the title tune and played a wagon train rider bringing settlers west through the deserts of Texas, New Mexico, Arizona and California.

In the "Flame of Araby" with Jeff Chandler and Maureen O'Hara, Lon Chaney, Jr. and I played the villainous Barberos Brothers.

In "Big Sky," made in Montana with Kirk Douglas and Elizabeth Theret (a full-blooded Cherokee), I played the role of Ahkim, a French Canadian trapper and all-around mountain man. I thoroughly enjoyed working with the large Indian cast in this picture, and became a good friend of two Blackfoot chiefs - Rueben Blackboy and Theodore Lonestar. Blackboy was 86, Lonestar 90, but they looked many years younger and rode their spirited steeds, bareback, as if they were nineteen. When we were packing up, getting ready to go home, they asked if I would remain behind for a day to be inducted, with full ceremony, into their tribe as an honorary member. I did, and it is one of my most cherished memories.

"Fair Wind to Java," with Fred MacMurray and Vera Ralston, was the last of the epic-scale pictures in which I had a major role. In between, I made a romantic comedy, "Dream Wife," with Cary Grant, Deborah Kerr and Walter Pidgeon. That went over so well that I was cast in another light-hearted vehicle, "Two Tickets to Broadway," with Janet Leigh and Tony Martin. By then, television was turning Hollywood upside down as the studios switched more and more of their production to scaled-down dramas for the little screen, and I decided to swim with the tide. That meant getting into television myself.

In the meantime, May and I were having our troubles. She wanted me to practice in front of a mirror for three hours every day. I thought it was unnecessary. She wanted me to keep my weight to around 265 I agreed that I should, but I didn't, sometimes zooming up to 290 before going on a crash diet. More importantly, she began to feel that she was carrying a disproportionate amount of our financial load, that I wasn't working as hard as I should, that I was letting too many opportunities slip by. She also began to see me as an alien interloper in her social world. I wasn't one of them. We decided, in 1957, to call the whole thing off.

Ed Sullivan and Steve Allen thought I fitted very nicely in their television world. I was a guest four times on each of their programs after May and I parted. By then I had become reasonably proficient as a dancer, having taken lessons in Hollywood, so I was able to add a nice soft-shoe and a few quick steps to my singing routine. This led to appearances on the Damon Runyon Show and the Jane Wyman Theater. Then I had a call from a major TV producer in Germany, and off I went for eighteen months to Europe.

The project was to produce 39 episodes, each to run a half-hour, on the adventures of Norwegian explorer Leif Ericksen, played by Jerome Courtland and produced by the Kirk Douglas Corporation and United Artists Studios. I played Leif's right-hand man, protecting his backside at all times as we ventured into various unknown parts of the seas and the world. My handy-dandy weapon was a heavy, carved figure of a woman. In an emergency, I grabbed "Little Maid" - as I called it - by the legs and brought it crashing down on the skull of the enemy. I spilled a lot of blood in that series, and saved Leif's life many times, so that eventually he could make his most famous voyage - the discovery of the New World. Unfortunately, the American television audience doesn't know about my contribution to history, for the series was never shown here. I can't understand why. It was very popular in Europe and Asia.

When "Tales of the Vikings" was finally completed I went to France to make a film called "The Bashful Elephant." The story revolved around a little girl and her parents who were struggling to make a living with their own traveling carnival. The bashful elephant was a part of their show, and, I hesitate to say, its star. I played the guy who managed the carnival and made sure we kept our engagements, despite storm, strife, and uncooperative minions of the law. I was no competition for the elephant, who stole the show. The studio made the picture in France because one of the biggest scenes was to take place at the palace in Versaille. It was easier to bring the cast to the palace than to build a replica in Burbank.

Throughout my stage and screen activities, Max and I remained as close as we had been during our boxing days. But for the first time in our lives we were not together. He missed that very much, and so did I. He kept in touch through a steady stream of letters. I saved two - the last two he was to write. I was in Germany at the time. They suggest his feelings in the closing days of his life.

October 26, 1959. "Dear Brother Buddy. Sickness seems to come in bunches. Dear Dad Sullivan was buried last week and the day before Aunt 'Jo' Phinney from across the street died. Ancil

Hoffman had a severe attack - they thought it was his heart. It was on the day he was to leave on a trip around the world. Lucky he wasn't on the boat, because Bob Harris couldn't have taken care of him. Mary is thinner than she ever was, taking care of her father and watching him slip away, not being able to hold on to the dear old man.

"Bernice told Mary your heart is giving you trouble and that you are in bad health. Is she correct? We both have to take off weight if we want to live a long time. So Buddy, take heed.

"I just got back from Toronto, New York, Washington, D.C., and Asbury Park, Long Island, where I refereed. Did Masquerade party on 20 August. Came home the 26th, then on September 24th went to Albuquerque to referee Joe Brown, lightweight champ, and wrestling two days later, then flew to Dallas, then Lubbock, and Amarillo, then home. So I punch out a few dollars here and there. Max, Jr. is in the Air Force. Send him a card!

"Stay well, chin up, watch diet, keep punching, watch out for the broads, don't drink, watch smokes, don't worry, and for heaven's sake send us a letter. Love and hugs always - Your old brother, Max."

October 27, 1959. "Dear Brother Buddy. I am happy for you that you have thirty-six half-hour Viking films in the can. Unless you are going to make another series of films, I'd use sound judgement and fly back to California. No use spending the money living in Munich, waiting for another job.

"Doesn't the Kirk Douglas outfit pay for your transportation? All other studios do when you go on location. Don't let them push or take advantage of you. There are more pretenders in show business than in any other business in the world.

"Can't you find a moment of time to write? Have your German secretary do it for you?

"How is the night life there. Is there any talent from America? Who is the biggest in show business there? How big is the cover charge, if any?

". Well Buddy, don't waste your time in Germany if you have no contract. We'll find a show of our own, here.

"Have you written Max, Jr.? I guess he broke his arm, we haven't heard from him in a month. But that's part of being young. There is no such thing as time when you are young. Stay well. We all love ya! Your old warrior brother, Max."

On November 21, I attended a party in Munich for a friend who had been working for Armed Forces Radio and was leaving for home. After the party I got in my car to drive back to my hotel. The battery was dead, for I had left the radio on all evening. I borrowed a battery to start the car. As soon as I hooked up, the radio came on. Armed Forces Radio reported, "We have just learned that American boxer Max Baer has died in a Los Angeles Hotel."

I disconnected the borrowed battery, backed up, moved forward, backed up again, and moved forward again. It was senseless, but so was the announcement. "What is Max up to now?" I asked myself in a daze. "This time he has gone too far." I sat in the car for several minutes, my heart racing, feeling light-headed and dizzy. Then I suddenly realized the report was on Armed Forces Radio. It must be true. Max was really dead.

In my confusion, I backed the car all the way to my hotel - a small place, a pensione. I had intended to back only into the street, and then drive forward in the normal manner. It seemed that I had lost my mind completely. In the lobby I asked the clerk - in perfect German which until then I had learned to speak only haltingly (had I lost my mind, or was it simply on another track?) - if he could get the American telephone operator for me. My brother had died. I wanted to talk to my sister, Bernice, who lived in Sacramento, near Max's home.

Bernice uttered a long, low-pitched scream. She hadn't heard the news. Neither had Frances in San Leandro. How strange, and awful, that I in Germany should be the first in our family to receive that terrible information. Mary knew, but she was still in shock, and hadn't called anyone else.

Max had never been ill from disease in his life. He had no history of heart trouble. He had medical check-ups on a regular basis. But he died from a heart attack that hit him as he was shaving in his room in the Hollywood-Roosevelt Hotel. He was on his way home from another tour of refereeing jobs in the western states, and had stopped over in Hollywood to do a television commercial. When he first felt the chest pain, he called the operator and asked for a doctor. "I'll send the house doctor," she said. "I don't want a house doctor, I want a people doctor," he responded with a laugh - so the operator explained afterward. Max quickly finished his shave, then lay down on the bed. The doctor arrived promptly and was applying the stethoscope on his chest when Max cried out, "Oh God, here I go." He was dead at age 49 -three months short of his 50th birthday.

Down through the years since that day I have been asked, over and over again - by reporters, people at work, people in show business - whether Max's boxing career contributed to his sudden death. Had he been hit too many times on the head? Was his heart enlarged? At the time, all of our family wanted the same information - me in particular, for I had taken some mighty wallops on the noggin. But the doctor told us he could find no abnormality in the heart. The autopsy report concurred.

Yet I still wonder. There is little family history of heart trouble. Dad died of Angina at age 63, Mother of cancer at age 60, but our grandparents lived normal life spans and our sisters are still going strong in their '70s and '80s. If it weren't for injuries that had nothing to do with boxing, I'd still be in great shape at 69. So, I still wonder if the autopsy report missed something.

His funeral in Sacramento was one of the biggest ever held in that city, and the most cosmopolitan of all. Women in diamonds and bums in rags, politicos and captains of industry and men of the ring, actors and musicians, rank and file people of every color and nationality all joined together to silently express their appreciation of Max. I wasn't there - I had been persuaded that there was nothing I could do if I came home, that I probably would miss the services - but Bernice tearfully recalled the impact of the funeral on her mind and feelings: "So many people of different races and religions, poor people and rich people. Oh God, why can't we all learn to love each other in life as we sometimes seem to in death." To which I add, "Amen."

Without Max, life for me could never, ever be the same. We were not joined together at the hip, but emotionally we were Siamese Twins. I didn't sing for several months.

LADY LUCK DROPS HER HANDKERCHIEF

There are times when I feel that all of my life has been compressed into a single moment. I felt that way when Max died. A tumbling assortment of images pushed the present from my mind. Max's fighting faces danced before me impish against Uzcudun, sardonic against Carnera, cruel against Schmeling, perplexed against Braddock, laughing against Levinsky, frightened against Louis, sad against Schaaf. A beautiful human face, so honest and expressive, so joyful, so alive that months after his death. I hadn't yet accepted it.

Memories of Max assumed a reality that encapsulated time. Thousands of yesterdays crowded into the then and now. Again I felt like a child, looking up to my big brother. Again I sat beside him in the farm truck. Again I felt a twinge of hurt at forever being labeled "Max's little brother." Again I felt an overwhelming surge of pride as I stood in the Oakland Tribune newsroom, watching the ticker tape tell of Max's destruction of Schmeling. The past had become present. There was something vaguely religious about it, for I was touched by an elusive glimmer of understanding that some way or another life is continuous.

The year was 1960. I was age 45. Would my career in movies, TV and singing hold up? I wondered. Should I play it safe and edge into a more durable type of work, at the same time holding on to whatever entertainment jobs I could get? What kind of job would allow me to be both an entertainer and a businessman? I had just started to consider the possibilities when the phone rang. An old friend from Oakland wanted me to have lunch with him at the Senator Hotel. When lunch was over, I was ready to start a new career. It was as if the Clark Equipment Company had intercepted my thought processes and tailored a job to suit my exact needs. I would be their public relations representative, helping to open doors to potential customers for their line of advanced technological hardware.

It mattered not to the company that I might be called to Hollywood or New York for a film or a singing engagement. In their eyes, that would enhance my value, for the bigger my reputation, the greater my influence might be. A sweet deal, I thought - and it was.

My territory was the western United States. I found, to my delight, that I could oftentimes combine daytime business for Clark with nighttime singing. I had just finished a short singing engagement in Los Angeles and found myself free one evening. I was staying at the Hyatt House West, near the airport, and decided to drop into the cocktail lounge where a pianist by the name of Vicki Farrell was performing. I would like to claim that it was the brainiest thing I ever did. But it was sheer luck.

Lady luck drops her handkerchief / 279

I asked for a table near the piano. At first, I was all ears. Rarely, if ever, had I heard such sophisticated sound from a single musical instrument. Old songs came alive. Here was a pianist who didn't need a singer to make words with her music. Then I opened my eyes as well as my ears. Vicki Farrell was gorgeous.

A cascade of glittering arpeggios, shifting from key to key, splashed happily into B flat and a haunting resurrection of "You and the Night and the Music" - a song that was popular in the thirties. "Does she always play like this?" I asked myself, "or is she inspired?" As she brought the tune to a whispering fadeout, she nodded to a waiter who immediately went to her side and bent over to hear her message. She looked squarely at me as she spoke. The waiter also glanced quickly at me, then said something into her ear. I almost popped a button. It was clear. She had asked about me.

A moment later she rose from the piano and walked toward the woman's lounge, a path that took her within a few feet of my table. As she passed, she dropped her purse, spilling several items - including a handkerchief. If I had been as fast in my fights with Joe Louis, he never could have beaten me. I think I went over the table in my haste to reach the purse. But my grace didn't match my speed. I managed to spill the remaining contents of the purse and was trying to stuff everything back in when she uttered a lilting laugh and said, "here, clumsy, let me do it." I gave her everything except the handkerchief. "My name is Buddy Baer," I heard myself say. Your picture in the lobby doesn't do you justice. You're the best pianist I've ever heard. I'll get you another handkerchief if you'll let me keep this one."

She said. "That would give me pleasure. I'm Vicki Farrell. You can pay for the handkerchief by singing a song when I come back." And off she went. "Lordy, Lordy," said I to me, "is this gal for real, or am I in heaven?"

Buddy's Lucky Lady
Vicki

Buddy was happy
meeting Vicki

I had sung at some of the best supper clubs in the country and had long ago gotten over my stage fright. Tonight, I was a novice again. Vicki set the mood of my song with an elegant introduction, and paused slightly for my entrance. I squeaked like a teenager. The audience laughed, thinking I was being funny. Vicki repeated a few notes to give me a new start. This time I croaked some kind of a baritone noise. Vicki smiled, glanced up at me and whispered, "you <u>are</u> joking, aren't you?" I gratefully agreed, and said I was really ready. The song went well, partly because of a tremolo I didn't know I had. It was born of fear. I was afraid that I wouldn't come up to Vicki's expectations. The other people didn't matter.

We had midnight supper, after Vicki had finished playing. I told her that she was an old fashioned romantic, and showed it by dropping her purse. She said I was equally romantic for wanting to keep her handkerchief. I agreed that I had a romantic streak in me, but it was very much up to date. Would she spend the night with me? "Buddy Baer," she answered with a wry smile, "it is still possible for Los Angeles to produce an old fashioned girl, and I'm one of them. Besides, I don't think you mean it. You are just testing, because that's supposed to be the way big he-men behave. Right?"

"Wrong," I said. "I suggested it because I couldn't help myself. Big he-men become ninety-pound weaklings in your presence, and I'm one of them. My mother taught me better, but she didn't tell me I'd meet someone like you." She smiled sweetly this time. "Thank you, Buddy. I'd be a fool to believe you, but it would be nice to pretend. I'll be back here tomorrow evening. Will you?" I saw her to her car. And I returned every night until my business in Los Angeles ended, and I flew off to Seattle. We were thinking about marriage.

I had told Vicki about my previous marriages to Ralpha Pearl, Ruth Boyington, May Mann and Doris LaVerne Conn. I assured her that I finally knew what I wanted and that she was it. "I'm a late bloomer in the emotional department," I said. "Give me a chance to prove it." I explained that only three of my marriages failed, because the match with Doris Conn wasn't consummated and ended in an annulment. I had met her at a time when I was feeling sorry for myself. We eloped to Reno. On the way back to Sacramento, immediately after the wedding ceremony, we had an argument and I took her to her families home rather than to mine. We never saw each other again. "I believe you," Vicki said. "When we marry, I think it will be for as long as we live, in sickness and in health and all that."

We couldn't marry as soon as we wanted because Vicki had filed for divorce from her only marriage, and had to wait for it to become final. She told me about herself. She had been born Verna Jewel Brumbelow, near Los Angeles, and was musical from the time she could reach a piano keyboard. Her professional career began when she was 16 and played both as a soloist and accompanist for the Kiwanis Club, schools and various social groups. Her voice teacher hired her to be his accompanist. About this time she changed her name to Vicki because it sounded more musical. Then she won the job as official accompanist for events staged or supported by the City of Los Angeles, such as the Hollywood USO, concerts in the park and special events. "Much prestige, little money," she said. So she began to perform as a cocktail pianist, first at the Imperial Gardens - a fancy place on the Sunset Strip - and then at the Hyatt House West. May the Hyatt House forever prosper. Without that fine establishment, we would not have met and, nineteen happy years later could not have toasted ourselves for knowing exactly what we wanted.

In 1965 I made my last TV movie - a western with Chuck Connors called, "Night of the Tiger." But I continued to sing, sometimes for profit, most of the time for fun. I still do. Vicki introduced me to her church, the Reorganized Church of Jesus Christ of Latter Day Saints. The church believes that music is good for the soul, so we perform together frequently.

Shortly after Max's death, the Fraternal Order of Eagles set up the "Max Baer Heart Fund." I am, and always have been, the national chairman for the fund, which over the years has raised more than $5 million for research in heart diseases. Fortunately, the Eagles also believe that music is good for the heart as well as the soul, and Vicki and I are invited to perform at many big state and national meetings of the order. Life is good.

Boxing critics used to say that I was too naive to survive in the boxing game. I shouldn't be let out alone at night, or someone might steal the clothes off my back, it was said. It was partly true. I never recognized boxing as a business. To me it was just fun so I never made any money out of it. But I did have sense enough to leave before the Baer brain had been banged and bruised into insensibility. My business acumen in the world of entertainment was just as lacking as it had been in boxing. By Hollywood standards, I was modestly paid for my movies. But I have never shared in any of the profits made by film companies on hundreds of reruns of pictures in which I appeared. That is true for most actors of the time, though many of the big names were able to secure residual rights in their contracts. The strike by Actors Equity in 1981 was one of the most justified work stoppages in American history, and as a result, today's actors will benefit by reruns - along with the producers.

I closed out my working life as an assistant sergeant at arms for The California State Senate. I took the job in 1976 and would still be there if I hadn't fallen off a stage at a senate hearing in San Francisco nearly three years ago, injuring my back to the point of disability. The world of the senate was a totally new world for me. I had never paid serious attention to the major social issues in California or anywhere. Hearing those subjects debated by men and women of considerable knowledge and wit fascinated me. Moreover, I discovered that the life of a senator -of all the legislators - was about ten times more work than play. It's never too late to learn, and I salute them.

REFLECTIONS

Looking back, I see lots of "it might have been," but only two have ever caused me any anguish. It doesn't bother me that at age 69 I am not a millionaire lounging about his pool on a palatial estate, as would have been possible if I had managed my life a little better, because I am happy and the beneficiary of a great family, a loving wife and many good friends. Money couldn't improve on that. I know that I should have finished high school, at least, but the fact that I didn't is not one of my great regrets. I lost my beautiful little bar in Sacramento - it would be a comfort to have it now - but I did go on to much more exciting work in films, and besides, the developers and "progress" would have gobbled it up anyway.

What does gnaw at me still is the lost championship of the world. Being absolutely honest with myself, I know it is not idle dreaming to believe that my first fight with Joe Louis was stolen from me by the powers that controlled the American boxing world in 1941. I have explained the reasons why I feel this way. Unlike my automobile accident a year later, which rendered me unfit to meet Louis a second time, the theft was not the consequence of fate. It was human connivance, born of greed.

The other crossroad in my life that causes me to wonder if I made the right turn is the use I have made of my singing voice. I never really made a decision on whether to study singing seriously, and give up boxing. I just drifted with the current. In 1935, when I was still a teenager, the famous New York sportswriter, Paul Gallico - later to become a novelist of consequence - wrote a column about my singing potential. Until then, it had not occurred to me that I might be able to make a living with my voice. I was flattered by what he had to say, but the picture he painted seemed too unreal to believe. Max was the world champion. I was his brother, following in his footsteps. How could life be any better?

That column by Gallico is in my scrap book - one of the few clippings I still have from my boxing days (the others, filling a small trunk, were stolen from my dressing room while I was making "Quo Vadis" in Rome). Gallico told of an evening he spent at our training camp in upper New York. Max and I and a friend had just returned from a movie. Several others, including Ancil Hoffman, were in the room. Max surprised everyone by saying he was going to bed. "I mention it," Gallico said, "because when Max Baer is eye-witnessed going to bed at 10:30, that's news." The column continued:

"Max held the floor for a while, while Buddy sat in a rocker with his sketch book. Buddy likes to draw. Max was saying that a year changes people an awful lot. 'Gee,' he said, 'when I think a year ago I had the nerve to step out on a stage and SING!!! I wouldn't do it now.' Then he said, 'but you ought to hear Buddy sing. Have you heard Buddy?'

"Politely we asked Buddy to sing. Buddy, six feet 4 in height, tremendous in bulk, powerfully built and muscled, but with a young, boyish face, put down his sketch book quietly without protest or false fuss. The valet went to the piano, and the talking died down a little, but not entirely.

"And then this big, burly young novice prize fighter began to sing, and suddenly there wasn't a sound in the room until he had finished. When he had, I let out a yell. Untrained, unschooled, singing from memory, the kid unloosed in the big Victorian parlor a magnificent and thrilling baritone as rich in quality and potentialities as any of the finest singing voices I have heard. It was rich, full, and had magnificent timbre. It was no crooner's or parlor singer's voice, but a real man's instrument, and even though untrained, still thrilling and stirring in certain registers.

"Max Baer, who adores his younger brother, said: 'Well, what do you think?' When he had finished, I said: I think he's a sucker if he ever laces on another glove. With a gift like that he doesn't have to be a prizefighter.' Ancil Hoffman looked shocked. He is nursing Baer along to be a champion. Buddy blushed. We asked him to sing more. He sang three or four ballads and showed that his first song was no accident, and that he really has something. Then he grinned and sat down to his sketchbook again. He has talent for drawing, too, but not to be compared with the natural gift for song, and the amazing instrument that has been given to him

"After Max went up to bed, I went over and sat down beside Buddy, and talked to him. He is a charming kid. He loves to sing. He has never had a lesson. He intends to study when he gets back to the coast. His fighting is to provide the money. He cannot read a note, but memorizes instantly. He can come out of a picture theater or a show after hearing a song and sing it through. He has talent for imitation and acting, too. He realizes, too, that if he could study and train his voice he would have something that would last him the rest of his life, and bring him a fine income twenty or thirty years after his days as a prizefighter are over. He knows no languages, but he would pick them up quickly because he is intelligent. I tried him on a German phrase, and he picked up the pronunciation immediately. What a magnificent figure of a singer he would make.

"But there is another side to the story, too. If Buddy stays in the ring for two or three years, his voice will be destroyed. One tough fight is liable to do it. Have you ever talked to a fighter who has been in the ring any length of time? They all have husky, breathy, guttural voices. Vocal chords were not meant to be punched. Nor will rattled brains and sluggish reaction help any man in any profession. Five years in the ring will make Buddy Baer a prizefighter with his future behind him. Five years of musical study and education will make young Baer a singer with his future before him, with perhaps - who knows - a world reputation. Which will it be? Buddy doesn't know. He is shy and excited about his voice. Perhaps if Champion Max really loves his kid brother he will take the padded mittens away from him and turn him loose in the brighter, better world of music. What a story that would be - a prizefighter turned into a concert singer. And how I would love to write it."

I have thought about that column a lot. What if Gallico knew what he was talking about? Should I have followed his advice? If I had, and had I achieved what he thought I could, would I have been as happy in the concert world - probably the opera world as well as I was in lighter musical settings? Maybe not, but I suspect that I was better suited temperamentally to be a singer of some kind than a boxer. If I had undergone the rigorous training Gallico advised, I'm sure I could have found major roles to play in musical comedy with an occasional foray into opera. Can't you just see me as Mephistopheles?

Boxers are special people. I liked-all of the fighters I met, in the ring and out. I found them to be more generous and outgoing in their friendliness than most other people. If you're down on your luck, and lucky enough to run into a boxer, chances are you won't go hungry. Some boxers I know gave away almost as much as they earned -Max being a prime example. I'm happy and proud to have been part of the boxing scene. As the song says about show business, there is no business like the boxing business. With all its faults, nothing can beat it for excitement, for its international cast of colorful characters - in the ring, in control of the ring, and around the ring in the form of millions of fight fans, of whom I'm still one.

As I end this story there is new public pressure to ban boxing. Several fighters have been killed in recent years. Many more have had their brains scrambled. I for one am not convinced that disease alone is responsible for Mohammed Ali's current inability to speak as fluently as he did in his prime. Yet I have little respect for doctors and others who would make boxing, alone, illegal for humanitarian reasons.

How about football? Over the years countless players have died from violent contact. Injuries are likely to be more severe than slurred speech - paralysis from the waist down or the waist up, for example. But I've heard no outcry to make the game illegal.

Auto racing is hardly bloodless. I have the feeling that a large percentage of the 500,000 people who attend the Indianapolis 500 race every Memorial Day weekend would be let down if there were not at least one spectacular crash. After all, the race itself requires an announcer to say who's ahead, so what else is there to get excited about? Several people die every year in one auto race or another, but nobody suggests that it is too dangerous to tolerate.

The rules for all sports should aim at preventing serious injury. I can speak for boxing. Olympic rules seem to be working well. They produce victories based on true boxing skills. I do not know of a single lasting injury sustained in an Olympic match. Yet the winners stack up very well indeed with professional competition, as Ali and Sugar Ray Leonard have shown.

EPITAPH

Buddy (born June 11, 1915 in Denver, Colorado) did not live to see the turn of the century, nor did Vicki (born Verna Jewell Brumbelow December 1, 1925 in Lomita, California) but they had many happy years together in Sacramento, California. Buddy was outward going and friendly by nature. Vicki was gracious and friendly and showed musical talent at an early age. Buddy died July 18, 1986, and Vicki October 25, 1997. Their earthly remains are together at Oaklawn in Sacramento and their true spiritual beings are united and with us still."

MEMORABILIA

These photos mark many events in Buddy's life. Former president Harry S. Truman looks small beside big and little Baer. Buddy with Max and Max's children. Buddy with Bob Hope, Dolores, and Vicki. Buddy with Fred Mac Murray- Deborah Kerr- Robert Taylor- Victor Mc Laglin- Jane Powell- Jimmy Duranty.

Buddy appeared in 15 films and here a few of the characters are captured including Ursus in Quo Vadis, and the Giant from Tales of Vikings.

A news paper photo shows Buddy knocking Joe Louis out of the ring.

Memorabilia / 295

Memorabilia / 297

Buddy Baer

You say in the headline that Buddy Baer knocked Joe Louis out of the ring in '41. Then in the story you say that Baer lost the fight when he could not answer the seventh-round bell. Would you tell this 19-year-old just who *did* win that fight?

        A. Gail Mandichak
        Burlington, N.J.

Louis did. Baer dumped the champ on his head in the first round (above). "But, dammit," says Baer, "he got back in." Baer lasted for six rounds and then was disqualified when his handlers, claiming a foul by Louis, wouldn't let him leave his corner.—ED.

www.ingramcontent.com/pod-product-compliance
Lightning Source LLC
LaVergne TN
LVHW021800060526
838201LV00058B/3183